The Codependent Therapy

Recovery Guide to Relationship Codependency for independent thinking and No more addiction.

Table of Contents

Introduction

Chapter One: Codependency Decoded

Chapter Two: Signs You Are In A Codependent Relationship

Chapter Three: Why It Is Important to Place Yourself First

Chapter Four: Recovery

Conclusion

Introduction

Congratulations on taking your first step to freeing yourself from the unfortunate shackles of codependency. This book is packed with loads of practical information, valuable tips and actionable strategies on not just identifying codependency but also breaking free from it to lead a more rewarding, gratifying and fulfilling life.

There are plenty of workable strategies and effective techniques that you can apply immediately to improve the quality of your relationships and develop greater self-confidence. By going through this book and following all the strategies, you're on your way to breaking free from the trap of codependency. Read the book in its entirety. Implement the techniques to bring about the positive changes in your self-esteem, sense of self-worth and life in general.

Chapter One: Codependency Decoded

What is codependency?

Much like other psychological concepts, codependency can be highly complex and confounding. Far from being another psychological or emotional health fad, it is a serious issue that is causing several relationships and lives to breakdown. It isn't just another feel-good, pop psychology concept but a real, tangible personal and relationship disorder that can consume the quality of one's life. It isn't another smart mechanism for mental health marketers.

If you've watched the movie, *Sid and Nancy,* you'll know what codependency is all about. It portrays a damaging love affair between bassist Sid Vicious (of real life Sex Pistols band) and his partner Nancy Spungen. When Sid begins a relationship with Nancy, his drug abuse spirals out of control. The film depicted the compulsions of these two addicts to be in a relationship despite clearly seeing how damaging the relationship could be for both. This pretty much sums up codependency. You may realize that the relationship isn't good for you but you're addicted to it and just cannot gather the courage to quit.

Another example of codependency is the tragic movie *Bastard Out of Carolina,* where the female protagonist is so damagingly and unhealthily dependent on her spouse that she is willing to sacrifice her daughter's physical and emotional well-being for it. The mother is in a relationship with a man who is unemployed and is constantly physically and sexually abusing her daughter. The woman repeatedly forgives her lover and believes him each time he promises not to do it again. This is a classic example of codependency.

What is codependency? Codependency in layman terns is relationship addiction or excessive dependence on other people to determine one's sense of self-worth, self-confidence, and self-esteem. The person needs constant approval, acceptance, and validation from other people to function smoothly. It is a psychological, emotional and behavioral condition in which an individual relies excessively on other people for their validation, worth, and identity.

A codependent association is marked by a person encouraging or causing his/her partner's excessive dependence or addiction, in addition to their undeveloped mental health, low accomplishments, irresponsibility, and psychological immaturity. It is an increasingly unhealthy dependence on another person for approval, which makes it dysfunctional. Codependency isn't just a barrier when it comes to enjoying healthy, positive balanced and fulfilling relationships, but also bit by bit destroys one's sense of self-esteem and making a person more susceptible to mental disorders and prevents one from leading a fulfilling, rewarding and gratifying life.

It is a mostly one-sided relationship where a partner is physically or psychologically destructive, whereas the other person in the relationship gets accustomed to the behavior sufficiently to not question or challenge it in any form. Codependents are overwhelmed by a compelling misconception that a person's self-worth stems from others.

Codependent was earlier utilized to refer to an enabler. Enablers were viewed as people helping addicts in their compulsive behavior by accepting complete responsibility for the addict, generally rationalizing the addict's behavior and preventing them from giving excuses. There is a propensity for denying the effects of the addict's dysfunctional behavior pattern. The term was first created by the Alcoholics Anonymous body and fundamentally focused on the issue of alcohol addiction, where the addict's family, friends, and well-wishers supported or led their addiction unintentionally or encouraged their dysfunctional behavior.

What causes codependency? In most cases, it is learned by observing the behavior of older family members. If we've grown up witnessing codependent relationships in the family during your childhood or adolescent years, there are higher chances of developing unhealthy relationship self-worth patterns. Children in households where both parents/partners share a destructive, unhealthy and abusive relationship reveal a higher inclination for codependent relationships. The witness, learn and internalize the destructive behavior patterns to adopt the same in their own personal relationships.

It breeds in an atmosphere where dysfunctional households refuse to identify or acknowledge the issue. Underlying causes such as shame, guilt, pain, regret, anger, and jealousy are often neglected and lay resolved within the subconscious mind. The issue can originate from addiction such as alcohol, gambling, smoking, gambling, and drugs or mental, physical or sexual abuse or chronic mental or physical illness. Rather than addressing and speaking about these conditions or eliminating them, the person reveals a tendency to repress the root problem.

The person suffering from any of the above conditions suppresses his/her emotions and disregards his/her need to convert themselves into a survivor. They get accustomed to living in denial or neglecting difficult to deal with emotions. They have trouble communicating their needs and detach themselves from the underlying psychological issue without confronting the issue. Lack of emotions and mistrust lead to underdeveloped psychological behavior and identity creation! One doesn't hold a balanced, positive and accurate view of themselves. Thus, children from dysfunctional households show a higher tendency for codependent behavioral tendencies within their personal relationships.

Codependency doesn't involve positive characteristics of emotions such as caring, fostering and nurturing a relationship. A positive, healthy and encouraging sense of care giving shouldn't be confused with codependency. Positive and balanced nurturing is a result of our choices and not compulsive or uncontrollable behavior patterns driven by our immature emotional state. Starkly different from positive caring and nurturing, codependency reveals a tendency to analyze the effects of a person's actions and nurturing for their needs. Positive, healthy relationships call for responsibility towards a person's sanity and well-being in addition to responsibility towards the relationship.

The definition of codependency is fraught with ambiguity and confusion. It isn't a straightforward or simple psychological concept that has several layers and behavioral aspects. Psychology experts hold the opinion that it is a preoccupation or obsession with other's problems to fulfill one's own overlooked emotional needs. Other psychologists and behavioral experts hint at codependency being excessive and unhealthy dependence on others, and their validation or approval to establish one's own identity.

Still, other experts are of the opinion that it is a relationship disorder where real, underlying issues about an individual's ability to relate to themselves are neglected. If you do not share a healthy relationship with yourself or find it challenging to relate to yourself at a deeper, emotional level, you lower your chances of enjoying healthy, rewarding and fulfilling personal relationships.

A more encompassing and widely prevalent definition of codependence suggests growing up dependent on a person who in turn depends on an aspect of that is non-dependable such as alcohol, nicotine, drugs, sex and overeating – anything that is done in excess or is compulsive.

A codependent individual is forever attempting to micromanage, fix and control other people's actions in a bid to flee from their own negative emotions, which they find challenging to acknowledge. There is a consistent pattern of picking partners who are addicts or substance abusers. The thing is – by focusing on what ails someone else allows codependents the comfort of shifting away focus from their own negatives.

They refuse to acknowledge what's wrong with them and compensate for it by constantly attempting to fix things for others to feel good about themselves. Also, they often get into relationships with the "needy" to ensure that their partners do not abandon them. They feed their partner's needs in a bid to keep them in the relationship. By focusing on the wrongs of others, codependents mange to overlook the unfulfilled void within themselves. They get into these damaging relationships to gain stability when the result is the exact opposite.

Let us look at an example of a codependent relationship. Since women are typically more prone to get stuck in a codependent relationship, we'll consider the typical relationship patterns of a codependent woman. Let us say Rose is almost always finding men who aren't keen on getting marriage and mention this to her in the beginning. Rose continues to overlook these early signs. She still takes up the challenge of getting the man to change his mind, win his heart and eventually marry him. This makes Rose hyper sensitive to any actions, emotions and behavioral patterns that show signs of rejection. In fact, Rose begins to expect it and feels unsettled when there are no signs of rejection. Once she experiences some form of rejection, she goes on to seek reassurance from the man that the rejection isn't true even though she's experienced it in past relationships. Reassurance is initially offered.

However, later when the man has to go on a business trip or dinner with friends, Rose becomes suspicious. She takes it as a form of rejection and believes her partner is avoiding her or cheating on her because she's just not good enough or doesn't deserve to be loved by someone like him. The demands then assume unhealthy proportions. Since the man has already mentioned at the onset that he isn't prepared to settle for a monogamous relationship, he perceives her nagging as over the top and isn't prepared to put up with it.

Slowly, Rose's partner starts pulling away from her. This makes her even more adamant and shrill about her demonstration of emotions. It isn't uncommon for such a tumultuous and unhealthy relationship to end on a disastrous note. Even in situations where the codependent eventually gets married to his/her partner, they will keep seeking reassurance of being needed, wanted and loved. At the core, there is an unhealthy desire to be needed all the time. Even marriage doesn't bring the security and reassurance codependents crave. In fact, it makes them even more clingy, needy and insecure.

The above mentioned example may have several variations. In some cases, the man may be insecure, apprehensive and dependent. It isn't uncommon for such an individual to turn into an alcoholic or substance abuser. If his partner is also insecure, anxious and apprehensive, she may enable his addiction simply to keep him in the relationship. Relationships between addicts and codependents are fairly common because both are able to feed off each other's needs for their sense of self-worth and emotional security.

Difference between dependency and codependency

Now that we have established a somewhat accurate understanding of codependency or codependent behavior, there may still be some confusion about the difference between interdependency or healthy dependency and unhealthy dependency or codependency. At times, interdependent people mistakenly pin down their behavior as codependency when it is merely a chase of regular dependence.

Let us consider some broad difference between codependency and dependency so a person can accurately determine if they are codependent or interdependent cloaking as codependent. These two forms of dependencies are distinct in the sense that codependent people are primarily dependent on others depending on them. Understand the paradox?

Codependency is viewed as a maladaptive, destructive and unhealthy trait that prevents people from enjoying meaningful relationships. On one hand, interdependent relationships are fraught with the two people relying on each for support, while understanding and caring for one another. It's an emotionally comfortable relationship where each person contributes towards the development and life of the other person for building them up and the entire relationship. Each person is self-sufficient and holds an identity as part of a twosome or any other association/relationship they hold.

In codependent relationships, there is an unhealthy dependency on others. People in a codependent relationship are unhealthily and destructively attached to one another. It assumes such proportions that their life goes off balance if they have to operate or exist by themselves. In a bid to fulfill their dependency requirements, they tend to suffer from a skewed identity, development issues and suppressed potential. They live in denial of their underlying fears, emotional issues, and self-doubt.

When you live in denial about core psychological issues, you eliminate the scope of overcoming them to live a more rewarding and enriched life. At the core of codependency lay several underlying and unhealthy emotional issues that need to be addressed to enjoy more meaningful relationships. On the other hand, in healthy dependency, there is no compulsive desire that your partner or another loved one clings on to you or is addicted to you to make you feel good about yourself. There is no need to sacrifice ourselves for our partner to reinforce our worth in our own or another person's eyes. In contrast to codependency, interdependent relationships are not laced with loneliness, insecurity, and unworthiness or perpetual quest of validation.

What makes codependency tricky is that it is learnt behavior that can be tracked to a person's childhood, where they've been subtly made to believe that their needs and preferences are not as important as that of the caregiver. The codependent person learns rather early in life that their preferences, needs, and requirements come after caregivers. They obtain a sense of value. The codependents may have attempted to assert their needs and desires at some point in time.

However, indirect or direct penalty as a consequence of this assertion may have led to their underdeveloped personality or the tendency to neglect their desires and wants over those of others. In their deeds and words, parents and caregivers enforce a compelling feeling of guilt towards your desires or term you selfish for articulating your needs and desires.

It is vital to note that your parents or caregivers may have had a history of addiction, stunted psychological growth and conditions of inadequacy. They compensate for their own sense of deprivation through a substitute abusive and unhealthy dependency on their children. Such parents perceive their children as being their caretakers, rather than them being the children's support, affection, and care system. At times, the parents may have utilized their children to compensate for the care, affection and nurturing they haven't received in their childhood. It is an unfortunate and vicious cycle that is challenging to break free from. This making up to the lack of affection in their own childhood ends up causing the children of these parents to pay heavily, making them codependents.

A majority of codependents constantly strive to be good children or go out of their way to be accepted by their parents (though the parents are seldom happy or satisfied with them). These children often do within their capacity to please their parents to seek acceptance and validation, which makes their parents' rejection all the more heart-wrenching for them. This feeling of rejection takes a toll on their sense of self-esteem, self-worth, and self-confidence, thus dooming them to a life of codependency.

A majority of codependents function with the belief (very early in life) that one has to be exceptionally good to be accepted by their parents/caregivers, or that they have to deny their own needs, requirements and desire to seek validation from the caregivers/parents.

One needs to give themselves up by forgetting their likes, desires, wants, emotions and preferences are the prime belief codependents operate with. They are internally programmed to internalize the belief that to be accepted, they have to keep their requirements secondary. The early emotional signs, experiences, and tendencies are typical for codependent people.

Folks in interdependent relationships do not demonstrate the tendency to place their needs after others. They are not programmed or conditioned to gain their sense of self-esteem or self-worth by staying subservient to their partners or perpetually giving sacrificing themselves at the altar of saving others. There is a positive, meaningful and healthy balance of adhering with another person's demands without giving up their own needs. The equation is one of mutual support, respect, appreciation, and understanding. One can comfortably demonstrate one's feelings and needs without attached guilt.

There is a normal reliance or dependency on the other person to fulfill your emotional requirements, which makes the relationship balanced, positive and healthy. When this dependency defines one's sense of self-worth, the problem arises. One can comfortably articulate their feelings, needs, and desires with an overpowering feeling of guilt. The dependency on the other person to meet your needs and expectations is healthy and positive. When this dependency negatively and unhealthily defines one's sense of self-worth is when the challenge arises.

Unlike codependents, people in interdependent relationships don't have difficulty asserting their needs and stance in relationships. They don't refrain from articulating their needs for the fear of being lonely, isolated and abandoned. There is a greater sense of sensitivity and responsibility for the other person's feelings, needs, and desires but not at the cost of their own feelings and emotions. There is always an attempt to find a middle way for the satisfaction of everyone involved.

A healthy interdependent relationship relies on a healthy give and take, where both parties function as equal rather a one person fulfilling the role of the giver and the other playing taker. In a positive, healthy and fulfilling interdependent relationship, an individual's emotions and actions are inextricably attached to their partner or the relationship. The relationship or partner doesn't become the be- all and end-all of their existence.

A huge difference between a normal interdependent and codependent relationship in that in the former, a person can normally function as an individual when seen as distinct from the relationship, whereas in a codependent relationship, the person doesn't have any identify other than the relationship, which becomes the focal point of their existence.

Dissecting the causes of codependency

Codependency is more often than not results from childhood trauma, growing up in dysfunctional families and witnessing a parent's/caregiver's codependent behavior while growing up. However, some dependents also claim to have perfectly normal childhoods. Yes, you may have had a perfectly normal childhood so to speak where your parents didn't get drunk, held towering expectations from you or beat you up.

There are several things that can happen when a child doesn't receive a stable, nurturing, supportive and positive home environment, which is one of the biggest causes of codependency.

When a parent is not capable of meeting the role of a parent, you may have assumed that role during your childhood; you may have taken the role of a caregiver and nurturer at home. This may have involved looking after your parents and siblings, stepping into the role of a bread winner, paying the bills, cooking food and doing household chores.

A codependent learns early in his/her life that people who confess their love for you may actually be out to hurt you. You may have been physically, emotionally and verbally hurt during childhood, parent/caregivers may have physically or emotionally abandoned you, family members may have threatened or lied to you, they may have exploited your large-heartedness or kindness for selfish purposes and other similar issues. Codependents grow up getting used to this feeling of being hurt be lovers, spouses, and friends. It becomes a pattern in their life. It is so deeply ingrained in the psyche since their childhood that they find it tough to question or break the pattern. It is almost normal for them, which, makes the entire process so unfortunate.

Codependents don't even realize until it is too late that there is a problem. Owing to their childhood experiences, they believe it is normal for people to treat them the way they do, at times even thinking they deserve to be treated badly. Even in instances of extreme physical or mental abuse, instead of blaming their partner for it, they will blame themselves and even believe that they deserve the abuse. All of this can be directly or indirectly attributed to childhood and early adolescent experiences within the family. When an individual's emotional needs remain uncared for over a period of time, they assume the form of a codependent personality.

Since codependents are almost left neglected or assume the role of a caretaker, they become people pleasers. Pleasing other people becomes the only way for them to hold control. They don't speak out or disagree with the other person out of a fear of hurting or offending them. There is a deep-seated tendency to please and be accepted by everyone that can be attributed to a tough childhood, where they were made to feel inadequate or were never seen to be 'good enough' for their parents/caregivers. Being a people pleaser feeds their sense of self-worth, and brings about a sense of emotional fulfillment.

Codependency is marked by an increased sense of guilt, where a person feels responsible for everything bad that happens to him/her or his/her loves ones even if wasn't caused by him/her. There is a deep-seated longing for wanting to rescue everyone and fix things for others. This may be a result of a feeling of helplessness and hopelessness at not being able to fix things in the family during their childhood years or not being able to rescue a family member being abused or ill-treated within the family. This growing sense of helplessness assumes an illogical and irrational tendency to fix things. The inability to fix things for your parents, siblings or family may have led to feelings of inadequacy that you try to overcome or compensate for by constantly wanting to rescue loved ones and fix things for them.]

Codependents lead a fearful and scary childhood, which translates into apprehensions, insecurities, and uncertainties during adulthood. They may not know what to expect. While some days may go smoothly, others may lead to anxiety, insomnia, nightmares, and depression owing to repressed fears and emotions. Feelings of being flawed, undeserving and unworthy are deeply ingrained within the codependent since childhood. You may be made to feel that the person who is mistreating you is never at fault but something is always wrong with you. The codependent believes this as a fact and doesn't attempt to challenge the notion. Being in a codependent relationship only reinforces this over and over again when they are bereft of any other reality.

Some adults who as children did not feel protected, cared for or attached to their caregivers feel an ongoing sense of insecurity that they continue to grapple with in their adult relationships. They operate with the belief that they are unwanted, often unsure of their attachment to other people, constantly worried or fearful of rejection or afraid that they will lose their loved one. If they find themselves with a partner who is inconsistent, unpredictable and abandoning, their fearful behavior will increase. Codependents become extra vigilant, focusing on resolving the problems of their loved ones. In their quest to prevent their partners from abandoning them or quitting the relationship, codependents tend to become angry, obsessive, jealous and over-possessive. They may take their quest for changing their loved ones or fixing things for them too far. In the process, codependents begin to lose themselves and turn lonely, hurtful and isolated. The term codependent came into being in the 70s and became commonplace while becoming a caricature term for passive victims of abuse, compulsive caregivers, controllers and enablers often assigned the blame for everything that goes wrong.

It may be possible that you've minimized, reduced or avoided acknowledging painful situations that occurred during your childhood. The codependency may be a defense mechanism or cover-up for all the painful things you've swept under the carpet or refused to acknowledge during your growing up years. It can be a result of emotional neglect by parents or caregivers. When our emotional needs aren't met during childhood, we tend to grow insecure, anxious and uncertain about other people accepting or considering us worthy of being loved, which manifests into codependent behavior. Another cause of codependency can be verbal, physical or emotional abuse. This can range from name calling, bullying, being given the silent treatment and threats. Downplaying problems is a huge sign of codependency. When you pretend something doesn't exist, you are showing indications of being a codependent.

Effects of being in a codependent relationship

Fear or inability to express yourself – A codependent person isn't able to express himself/herself freely since they are always operating with the fear of displeasing or upsetting the other person. You may not be able to articulate your needs freely, which is a huge challenge in any relationship. Bottled up and repressed emotions, feelings, and desires can lead to severe health issues such as depression and other mental disorders.

Neglecting one's needs – One of the biggest consequences of codependency is overlooking personal needs. This involves taking extreme measures to ascertain that the other person is not displeased or unhappy, often at the cost of your own happiness, sanity and well-being. Your needs become secondary to the other person, and there is an unhealthy balance where one person is completely neglecting their needs to ensure every need of the other person is met.

Cannot cope with being alone – Codependents often have an inherent need to latch on to others, even if it is at the cost of their own needs. Since they may not have received the required emotional comfort, care and affection in their formative years, they crave being wanted. They find it near impossible to be alone as there is a compelling, underlying need to look after or care for someone. This validates their existence or purpose of life. Codependents derive their sense of self-worth through others. This may lead them to form negative associations with wrong people, causing them even more emotional distress and damage. Instead of being alone, they prefer being in a relationship, irrespective of how damaging the relationship is to their well-being. It is precisely for this reason that they stay in emotionally, physically, sexually and verbally abusive relationships because leaving and being alone seems much worse than staying in a damaging relationship. Being needed in the relationship seems to validate their existence or in their mind is the only purpose of their life. Thus one of the most damaging effects of codependency is being in destructive and negative relationships that offer a further blow to your self-esteem, self-confidence, and sense of self-worth.

Not taking help – If you are codependent, you'll typically be ill at ease when others try to do something for you. The role of a caregiver or help giver is firmly embedded in your subconscious mind. This makes it tough for you to alter the equation and accept help from others. A situation where others try to offer help or care for a codependent becomes uncomfortable for them (codependents) since they believe this will make the other person grow resentful of them or hate them.

Being in a codependent relationship can lead to innumerable relationship troubles. For instance, a codependent person may give their all to a relationship. However, if the other person doesn't display the same sentiment, it can lead to the codependent person developing mental conditions such as depression and anxiety. This compulsive behavior to slip into the caregiver's role can also cause codependents to get into relationships where they are likelier to be hurt or their needs are completely overlooked.

Chapter Two: Signs You Are In A Codependent Relationship

Now that you know what codependency broadly encompasses, and the distinction between dependency and codependency, how do you know if you are stuck in the web of a codependent relationship? How do you determine if you are the victim of a codependent relationship? There are in thin line between distinguishing if you are stuck in a codependent relationship or one where there is healthy dependency of the other person's caring, affectionate and nurturing nature? What are the general characteristics of a codependent individual? Here are some important pointers for helping you determine if you are stuck in a codependent relation since indentifying it is the first step towards liberating yourself from such self damaging and destructive relationships.

Codependency is generally known as the condition of the "lost self." These relationships are mostly marked by dysfunctional communication, excessive dependence, complete control or dominance, and increased reactivity. Unlike popular belief, codependency isn't simply limited to romantic relationships (though the percentage is fairly high) but can also occur in numerous other relationships such as friends, parents, and co-workers. Understand that codependency has little to do with other people and more an 'internal fault'. It is a result of our faulty emotional and behavioral mechanism built over a period of time by neglecting damaging underlying subconscious feelings and emotions. When we exist and function in denial that these issues exist, it builds and prevents us from leading healthy relationships. The fundamental issue is of us placing our priorities, needs, and desires below others, and not so much about how other people perceive or treat us. It is about how we view and treat ourselves viz-a-viz other people in a relationship. Here are some typical underlying attributes of a codependent person.

1. Codependent people are perpetually stressed, worried and obsessed about how others, especially those they love or care for deeply, view them. There is a strong need to be approved and validated by others. Much of their identity is defined by the view other people hold about them. There is

a high premium of pleasing everyone, often at the cost of their own sanity, desires, and priorities.

2. People suffering from codependency or stuck in codependent relationships, often keep quiet to prevent confrontation despite realizing they aren't wrong. They duck logical or rational arguments for fear that the other person may become displeased or worse abandon them (their worst fear). They do not feel the need to assert themselves, and simply go with what their other person says or dictates, whether they disagree or agree with the person. There is a fear of relational arguments and analysis because somewhere deep within selves they realize the other person is wrong.

3. They are often subject to physical, mental and emotional abuse in a relationship. There is also a tendency to be belittled all the time by others whom they cling on to for emotional support and affection. Codependent people often get accustomed to being treated disrespectfully in a relationship.

At times, it gets so bad that they just cannot stay in a healthy, positive and respectful relationship. Instead of blaming their partner or family member, they blame themselves for being abused and humiliated all the time. They do not believe that being humiliated and abused at every opportunity is a real issue. In fact, they believe the issue exists with them and that no one else is responsible for corrective measures.

Sometimes, there is an excessive need to pamper the other person's ego at the cost of demeaning themselves. In many cases of physical, mental, sexual and emotional abuse, the codependent victim actually believes that they deserve to be humiliated, abused and hit. There is a damaging dependence on relationships, where a codependent goes to any extent to prevent being abandoned by the other person.

4. Codependents experience a high feeling of rejection when their partners spend more time with friends and peers. A positive, fulfilling and healthy relationship is one where both partners are comfortable taking time away from each other to nurture their individuality and enjoy time out with

friends. In a codependent association, one persona almost always experiences a feeling of rejection and loneliness when the other person spends some much needed alone time with friends and peers. They take it as a form of being rejected by their partner for not being good or interesting enough. There is an assumption that they aren't stimulating or exciting enough for the other person, which is why he/she spends more time in the company of friends. The codependent invariably equates this with not being good enough for the other person. There is an overpowering tendency to take every action of their partner personally.

Codependents forever doubt their abilities, while revealing an excessive need for acceptance and validation from others to increase their sense of self-worth or feeling capable. They are constantly held by emotions of inadequacy around who they want to be and what they desire to accomplish in life.

5. Codependents are seldom able to express or articulate their real feelings, hidden as they are under the blanket of trying to seek validation from others or please others. They have a hard time expressing their inner feelings and emotions. For example, if they desire greater physical intimacy within their relationship, instead of revealing their needs to their partner, they will simply avoid speaking about it. They do not want to displease the other person or come across as excessively demanding.

6. There is a greater tendency to see themselves as 'bad' or 'negative' people even when they make the tiniest mistakes. Emotionally balanced folks in fulfilling and healthy relationships possess a healthy tendency to separate themselves from their actions and perceive their actions as wrong or negative. However, codependents attribute each mistake with being inherently 'bad' people. They cannot get themselves to isolate themselves from their negative actions.

7. Some codependents are of the opinion that the lives of their loved ones will be completely affected and devastated if they don't care for them or look after their well-being. They experience a constant urge to play rescuer, cheerleader, and supporter of other people's lives, often leaving their own needs and desires neglected. These people fulfill their own emotional

requirements by depending on other people's inadequacy or malfunctioning.

8. Codependent people have an increasingly challenging time accepting compliments and other affectionate gestures from others. They seldom believe compliments directed their way, often thinking they aren't worthy of it and people are just offering compliments to make them feel good without actually meaning it.

They don't believe they are worthy of being pampered with nice gifts, gestures, and words. Codependents are so accustomed to being givers and giving up their needs that they find it challenging to believe they deserve anything at all or anyone should do anything for them. They hold too low an opinion of themselves to be considered worthy of receiving anything good or positive from anyone.

9. Codependents have trouble refusing people. They are largely people pleasers, who seek to make others happy often at the altar of their own desires, priorities, and needs. They gain an increased sense of validation by pleasing other people, often paying a huge price for it. There is a distinct inability to develop assertiveness and refuse when they aren't in a position to meet the other person's needs.

Codependents will go through discomfort instead of politely and assertively refusing the other person. Asserting themselves or articulating their needs induces a sense of guilt within the codependent. For example, even if they aren't ready for it, they may give in to the sexual demands of their partner, and mistakenly strengthen their intimacy.

10. Codependent individuals have increased trouble reaching out to others for help. They just don't have it in themselves to tell people they need support, encouragement, and help. They operate like they are holding the world's responsibility on their shoulders, and rarely seek help and assistance when it comes to their own desires and requirements. They assume the role of care givers, confidantes and nurturers to extremely unhealthy proportions by assuming that their responsibility is restricted to helping others and not seeking help. They often feel guilty about seeking

help and think it is their sole prerogative to offer help, support, guidance, and a shoulder to cry on.

11. Codependent folks generally take on plenty of tasks, which make it challenging for them to focus on a single task. They feel a compelling urge to do several things together just to feel good about themselves. This serves counterproductive to the purpose and only hampers everything they do, thus leading them to feel even more miserable about themselves. Their sense of self-esteem and self-worth further nose dives.

12. One of the biggest indications of a codependent is he/she almost always mistakes love for pity. There is a greater tendency to demonstrate affection towards or stay in relationships with people the codependents pity. They are generally attracted to people who they believe need rescuing. There is a total lack of a healthy give and take balance.

Codependents are either pitiable in their relationships where they are perpetually seeking sympathy from the other person or making extreme and damaging efforts for showering the other person with pity (or turning into their savior) often at the cost of their own needs and sanity. They have the tendency to fabricate stories and offer complicated explanations for hiding their true feelings and requirements. Codependents pick lying and being dishonest over stating the truth to avoid hurting or displeasing others. They believe in stating the truth in an honest and upfront manner will make the other person hate them. This is exactly why they have trouble calling out a spade because they lack the confidence to be assertive.

13 Codependents find it a huge challenge to make decisions, especially where they are concerned. They are so insecure, unsure and hesitant about themselves that they need constant validation and reinforcement from others to be sure of their identity. They do not believe in their ability to wield the right decisions and more often than not rely on others for making important decisions on their behalf. They'll need help even if it comes to picking an outfit for themselves, they are so unsure about their choices. The codependents sense of self-doubt, inadequacy and reduced self esteem comes in the way of sound decision making.

14. Another huge indicator of a codepodent is that they are hyper sensitive, emotional and vulnerable. Their fragile and wafer thin self-esteem tends to make them more reactive, sensitive, emotional and vulnerable to the tiniest trigger. The reactions often range from downright irrational to slightly unfounded. There is no concept of balanced reactions. Even regular suggestions, comments, feedback, and criticism are taken personally and seen as a personal attack by them. Since their sense of self esteem and self confidence is so low, they find it challenging to respond even to constructive criticism in a healthy and balanced manner. There is a tendency to take everything personally or perceive it as a direct, personal attack.

15. Codependents have the tendency to awfulize and exaggerate. This is especially true for people who've grown up in dysfunctional families and are conditioned to expect the worst. They grow up with a more negative, pessimistic and catastrophic view of the world around them, thus expecting the worst in any given situation. Even as adults they reveal a tendency to interpret things in a more exaggerated, catastrophic and pessimistic way. Even something positive is tinted with their own shade of negativity. For instance, if someone offers them a compliment that they are looking particularly good today, they may start wondering if they look ugly on other days. Get the drift? Codependents are almost always awaiting disaster. In fact, they are actively seeking it. This leads to a miserable chain reaction, where they create all that they fear or worry about. It doesn't happen at a conscious level but this is a mere cover-up for their lack of emotional skills and habits.

16. There is no concept for gray for codependents. They create an emotional web where everything is perceived as black or white. There is no in-between. Their emotions, feelings, reactions, and thoughts are extreme. Let's look at an example to better understand this point. Jack is a science professor who stumbles upon the information that some students aren't too satisfied with his teaching methods.

What will a balanced, logical and rational person do in such a scenario? He/she will speak to his/her students and solicit suggestions about effective teaching methods that work for them. They'll probably try different teaching approaches and gather feedback from students about what works best for them. A balanced person's primary objective will be to make the process of learning and teaching more effective. In contrast to this, if Jack has a codependent personality, he may quit the post and apply for a job at another institution. The criticism will be taken more personally, which may lead Jack to believe that "students hate me."

A typical characteristic of a codependent is that there isn't a room for alternatives, discussion or constructive action that works for everyone involved. For codependents, people either hate them or love them. There are no alternatives, and no in betweens! Do you indentify with this?

17. Predictably, codependents often face issues related to intimacy and bonding in relationships. While talking about intimacy, we are not merely focusing on sexual intimacy but in more encompassing terms. Intimacy isn't so much about being pinned down by pangs of fear and insecurity or being rejected, deserted and abandoned in a relationship. It is more about being able to express oneself and be open about your wants, needs, and desires in an intimate relationship. Codependents often struggle to express their internal emotions and feelings, which proves to be a huge barrier in their intimacy quest. Intimacy and close bonds are instead taken over by huge dependence. They view dependence and not healthy sharing of feelings and emotions as intimacy. Needing someone or being desperately needed by someone is viewed as intimacy in their eyes. Closeness and sharing of feelings or emotions are replaced with heavy dependence.

18. A codependent will do everything in their capacity to maintain a perfectly harmonious and balanced relationship. Answer these question carefully, do you find yourself forever adjusting your words, actions and feelings to maintain peace even in the face of the other person's anger and outburst? Instead of setting boundaries about how you deserve to be treated, do you go all out to curtail your reaction for maintaining an unhealthy act of normalcy? Instead of rectifying or calling out the other person's actions, you put up with it for fear of destroying the normalcy of a situation.

Do you closely connect with most of these potentially damaging and unhealthy symptoms? If yes, there are high chances you are a codependent or stuck in a codependent relationship. It may be the time to seek help from a licensed psychologist, therapist or psychiatrist who possess the expertise to treat codependency.

A codependent individual is someone who lets another person's behavior control or affect them, and who is obsessed with the idea of controlling the other person's behavior. The other person can be anyone from a romantic partner, spouse, sibling, parent, client, friend or grandparent. These are people we share close relationships with. The person is generally an alcoholic, suffering a physical/mental ailment, a drug addict or even a regular person who demonstrates sad feelings and emotions occasionally.

There can be various signs of codependency, a majority of which have been listed above in detail. Here's another quick list to help you identify if you are codependent. These are typical characteristics, traits, and symptoms of codependency. This is just a snapshot of what is a virtually endless list of complicated, interwoven traits stemming from multiple repressed, underlying feelings and emotions.

-They feel responsible for other's emotions, actions, thoughts, choices, feelings, wants, desires, needs, well-being, and fate. Everything that happens to those close to them is perceived by them to be a result of their choices and actions.

- Codependents experience a compelling urge to help a person solve their woes, which is fulfilled by offering unsolicited advice, offering multiple suggestions or trying to fix emotions and feelings.

- As a codependent, you may find yourself agreeing to do things you don't really want to do, which ends up with you doing more than what you can handle or are capable of doing.

- While codependents find it easy to express anger and displeasure about injustices meted out to others, they don't gather the same resolve when it comes to taking a stand for themselves. It is easier for them to speak up for others rather than for themselves.

-Codependents are attracted to needy people. They can't bring themselves to be in a healthy, balanced give-take relationship, where the other person doesn't desperately need them.

-They look at their relationships to give all the good they have, seldom keeping anything positive behind for themselves. Their positive feelings and emotions are almost always only directed at the other person.

-Codependents more often than not feel angry, manipulated, victimized, used, betrayed and unappreciated.

- They generally come from family set-ups where the healthy exchange of emotions and feelings isn't fostered. The families are often repressed, abusive, addiction prone and dysfunctional.

- Codependents blame themselves for everything that happens to others and themselves.

- One of the biggest signs of codependency is operating with a sense of inadequacy, a feeling of never being good enough or reduced self-worth as a result of childhood conditioning. There may have been instances where your parents had high expectations from you or were never satisfied with what you did, which lead you to believe that could never please anyone or aren't good enough for anyone.

- Codependents find it tough to accept compliments and praise in a healthy manner. They believe people are just being nice to them or outright lying because in their mind – they can never be good enough.

Warning signs you are in a codependent relationship

How do you know if you are simply over-possessive and afraid of losing your partner (which is commonplace in romantic relationships) or if you are in an unhealthily codependent relationship? There can be a thin line between a dependent and codependent relationship. Here's how to identify if you are in a codependent relationship.

Constantly covering your partner's shortcomings and limitations is a sign of codependency. If you are in a codependent relationship, you will almost always feel responsible for your partner's behavior. There is a tendency to feel responsible for their actions, behavior, and words. You may make excuses on their behalf, cover up for their irresponsible behavior and care for them in the face of their careless behavior (example constantly loaning them money when they aren't steady in pursuing a job or career). This is a typical sign of a codependent relationship, where you are always covering up and offering excuses for the other person's bad behavior even when you know he/she is wrong.

You are constantly worried that the other person will abandon you or leave. This deeply ingrained fear makes you do all sorts of things to put up with the other person's behavior despite knowing it isn't acceptable. You will do anything to maintain the relationship even when it's destructive. A codependent person will reveal obsessive and compulsive tendencies in extreme cases to prevent their partner from abandoning them.

One of the biggest signs of codependency is forever placing your needs secondary to the other person. A codependent will almost always push back their needs in a relationship. They will seldom express their needs, desires, and emotions, and often end up sacrificing it to accommodate those of their partner. As a codependent person, an individual places greater importance on their partner's well-being than their own. Their self worth is directly proportional to their ability to care for their partner. When their efforts do not work, codependents may get depressed.

Sacrificing your personal values for accommodating the other person's inherently selfish needs is a more or less definitive sign of being in a codependent relationship. Codependent people find it challenging to establish boundaries in relationships, which is why they will do just about anything to avoid their partner's displeasure and anger, often going to the extent of giving up personal values. For instance, a codependent person may desire love and emotional intimacy but may settle for sexual seduction or attention. They may give up their own desire for emotional needs to accommodate their partner's desire for sex. They may feed the addict's behavior in a quest to avoid displeasing them.

Constantly keeping tabs on their partner! It is one thing to ensure a loved one is safe, and another to stalk every move they make. This behavior assumes obsessive proportions in a codependent relationship, where you may find yourself constantly checking the other's phone, monitoring their activities, calling them incessantly to find out where they are to keep tabs over them. A codependent may stress about what their loved one does when away from them, and keep checking on their plans.

The codependent will avoid conflict at any cost even if it means acting passively around the addict. They may use everything from indirect communication to hiding their true feelings to prevent inciting their partner's rage, violence, and verbal insults.

There is a higher tendency for inflicting self harm in codependent relationships. The person may focus their control inward when outward control fails to work. According to research, there is a significant correlation between eating disorders and codependent relationships. This can assume other self destructive and damaging behavior.

Dysfunctional communication pattern is one of the biggest signs of a codependent relationship. As a codependent, you may have serious trouble communicating or expressing your feelings, emotions, desires and needs to your partner in a bid to prevent displeasing them. You may not want to bother them with your problems. Also, you may not be truthful when it comes to voicing your individual and independent opinion to avoid upsetting the other person. Instead of stating, "I really don't like it" you may pretend things are alright or not correct your partner's actions. Communication is misleading, dishonest, hesitant and confusing. You try to manipulate your partner from a deep sense of fear, uncertainty, and insecurity.

Narcissism and codependency

There is a close connection between narcissism and codependency, where codependents are often attracted to, and form intimate relationships with narcissistic type personalities. We know by now that codependency is a result of a lack of healthy relationships with the self (as a result of childhood experiences or repressed emotions). There is an unhealthy tendency to put other people's needs before theirs.

Much like codependents, narcissists also share unhealthy relationships with the self. They have the tendency to place themselves and their wants above everything else. Unlike codependents, they use other people for serving their own ends, often exploiting people and relationships to fulfill selfish objectives without accompanying feelings of remorse, regret or guilt. They are quick to pass blame on others and seldom view anything as their fault.

If you look at it logically, a codependent and narcissist coming together is filling each other empty spaces, much like jigsaw puzzle pieces being fitted together. One becomes an easy marker for another, and a deep connection is established. There can also be familial connections or links to this process. If one parent in the household displayed predominantly narcissistic tendencies, the child may grow up to be with either a narcissistic or codependent. Similarly, if both parents are narcissistic, again the child can turn into a codependent or narcissist. It becomes challenging for the codependent to stand against or set boundaries for the narcissist.

Several popular narratives will portray codependents as helpless victims at the mercy of manipulative narcissists. While there may be some amount of truth to this, it largely oversimplifies the basic fact that at their core both narcissism and codependency originate from an unhealthy perception of oneself. When you understand this basic fact, it becomes easy to think of both as two sides of the same coin instead of enemies. Though their behavior may be different, the needs that codependents and narcissists are looking to fulfill are similar.

For the codependents or any average person, it is tough to understand a person who totally lacks the ability to empathize with others and learn from earlier mistakes. The fundamental mistake of the codependent is to keep giving the benefit of doubt to their narcissistic partner because its challenging for them to digest that a person can be selfish, unyielding and manipulative to this extent.

Both narcissism and codependency are connected to an under defined self. The sense of self or self-worth isn't clear in both narcissist and codependents. Both often struggle to comprehend who they really are. People with both these tendencies rely on others to define or validate their identities. They place a lot of premium on what other people think about them or how they are perceived by others. This, in turn, determines their sense of self-worth or identity. While people demonstrating narcissistic tendencies intensely and exclusively focus on their needs (displaying complete lack of empathy, regard or sensitivity for other's needs), codependents are hyper focused on other people. Their identity is concentrated on being useful to and serving other people.

Narcissists often require other people to boost their sense of self-esteem in the form of continuous admiration. This makes them feel wonderful about themselves. On the other hand, codependents believe they know exactly what is good for the other person. Unlike narcissists who crave praise and admiration, codependents yearn for gratitude and 'being needed'. Think of it like this – almost everyone wants to feel needed and admired. Codependency and narcissism are taking it to extreme levels owing to underdeveloped emotions. Both conditions involve heavy dependence on other people's approval.

Codependents often form relationships with narcissists owing to their complementary roles that fulfill each other's needs and primary emotional goals. While the codependent partner finds something they can completely immerse themselves into, the narcissistic individual finds someone who is willing to put their (the narcissist's needs first). Thus the equation fits perfectly, though the relationship can be an absolute disaster.

The dynamics can turn unhealthy when the codependent individual tries to function vicariously through the comparatively stronger narcissistic partner. When the narcissist doesn't reveal too much gratitude for the codependent's care and service, he/she may begin developing feelings of pain and resentment. Similarly, the narcissistic individual may misuse their partner's pleasing tendencies to the hilt for fulfilling their own narcissistic supply. As the narcissist's ego expands (fed by the codependent), their desires and demands also increase. This happens until the codependent finally burns out.

There are cases where a narcissist and codependent may not want to leave a relationship even when it turns into abusive. Both parties may prefer living in an unhealthy relationship set-up or equation over quitting for fear of not feeding ego or sense of self worth. The fear of being alone drives plenty of codependents and narcissists to be a part of dysfunctional and unhealthy relationships. In the absence of intervention or professional help, the relationship can grow even more toxic with time.

At times, narcissism and codependency can overlap. They don't always have to be the opposite ends of a spectrum. How different is the desire or yearning to feel important and be needed all the time? While some research has proven that narcissism numbers among codependents are low, others have discovered higher narcissism rates among people displaying codependent traits.

Think of it like this. An individual who is codependent in a situation may be narcissistic in a different situation, their behavior originating from the desire to be needed or admired. For example, an individual may become codependent within a marriage, taking care of their spouse's needs. The same person may feel an overwhelming need for praise, compliments, and respect from their child, thus leading them to manifest more narcissistic characteristics.

In certain cases, an abusive person may gaslight a codependent person into believing that they are being narcissistic. The abuser can sabotage any demonstration of self-confidence as egoistical or narcissistic, and since codependents are so accustomed to taking everyone's views about seriously, they have no trouble believing their partner. Any act of self-care such as taking time off for oneself or enjoying with friends will be tagged as selfish. What makes it worse is, the codependent person ends up believing all these accusations, and attempts to fix the relationship by overlooking their needs. They start believing that it is indeed their fault, and that to save the relationship they should stop thinking about themselves. In the absence of isolation from loved ones or a more objective third person view, the codependent is likely to believe they are displaying narcissistic tendencies.

Since almost everyone reveals narcissistic or codependent tendencies at some point or another, it becomes even more challenging to determine if a person is narcissistic, codependent or a bit of both.

Codependency and jealousy

Much like codependency, jealousy also originates from a feeling of inadequacy, insecurity and a low sense of self-worth. When you don't consider yourself as good as your partner or someone you think your partner is flirting with or attracted to, sparks of jealousy and insecurity are bound to fly. This behavior assumes obsessive proportions when it comes to codependents because there is a deep psychological need to cling on to the relationship at any cost. To protect your relationship, you may go to any extent. There is a thin line between envy and jealousy. While envy stems from a desire to get something someone else possesses, jealousy is a deep seated fear of losing what's ours. In a codependent relationship, this can imply an underlying fear of being abandoned by your partner.

Codependents are highly vulnerable to losing their partner's attention or affection. They are often taken over by a type of mental discomfort owing to insecurity, suspicious, fear of a 'rival' snatching away their loved, unfaithfulness and other similar issues. It becomes even more marked when the codependent's perceived rivals have qualities they desire for themselves. Research reveals that people who have an insecure personality reveal greater jealousy. Thus, jealousy stems from an inherent feeling of inadequacy.

Let us say Rose suffers from a deeply held belief that is inadequate and not deserving of real love. This makes her purportedly solicit male attention and sometimes act in a manner that makes her partner jealous. Rose's jealousy also stems from her insecurity. She imagines that her partner desires other women, when that may not be the case, and constantly keeps a tab of his moves. Her beliefs are a direct result of a toxic and unhealthy internalized shame that isn't uncommon in codependents. It can be caused by psychological or emotional abandonment during formative childhood or adolescent years creating problems in the person's intimate relationships as an adult.

Let's contrast this situation with someone who boasts of a healthier and more balanced personality. Jane demonstrates a healthy sense of self-worth. She has a healthy and balanced opinion about herself. When her partner goes for lunch with his female friends and co-workers, she doesn't feel jealous or insecure. This is because she is sure of her relationship, and believes she deserves all the love. Even if Jane's partner does have an affair with his female friends or co-workers, she won't blame herself for it because she doesn't believe that her partner's affair is a reflection of her inadequacy. In short, she won't blame herself for it, unlike a codependent person who will blame themselves for their partner's actions. Of course, there will be a fear of losing the person or a loss of a relationship. However, it is more a wake-up alarm that there are unresolved things that need to be addressed by the two partners.

Codependency and addiction

Again, codependency and addiction form an unfortunate association that is challenging to break free from. Codependency happens when a person who isn't addicted to substance, alcohol, food or other addictions is controlled by the addict's actions. In simple words, the codependent is addicted to a relationship with the addict. Though like we've discussed in earlier chapters that codependency is generally developed during childhood and adolescent years by observing the behavior of caregivers within the family or by repressing negative emotions and feelings, it can also originate from perfectly normal behavior.

Codependency can begin with caring for a person, wanting to be helpful, being more compassionate towards an addicted partner and desiring to trust them. These are common intentions of people in relationships. However, when this behavior takes extreme form and you start indulging in enabling behavior is when the problem begins. The codependent then promotes sickness and addiction, both in their partner and themselves, thus giving the relationship an unhealthy twist.

Codependency and addiction are closely connected because codependency was initially used to imply intimate relationships with alcoholics. Even today, addiction is linked to codependency. Addicts almost always have deeply embedded psychological and emotional issues that haven't been resolved. This can be anything from monetary issues to relationship woes. The codependent partner may do their best to support the loved one through their ordeal. However, these may be just on the surface gestures to help the addict heal without going to the root of the problem. More often than not in a bid to offer them temporary comfort and avoid displeasing them, the codependent may actually help the addict indulge in harmful acts, then clean it up and cover up for them. They may lend the addict emotional, financial and other support to continue their addiction.

Though codependency isn't linked with addiction in all cases, there is a mostly a codependent for addicts. The most unfortunate thing is, in several cases, the codependent often practices addictive behavior. It is possible that both people may demonstrate codependent behavior tendencies. In such a scenario, one individual will have more severe issues than the other, while the other person assumes the role of a supporter and caregiver.

There are generally two sides of a codependent relationship. One person plays the manipulator, while the other becomes the enabler. In cases of addiction, the person engaging in abuse becomes the manipulator who controls the codependent's actions through their emotions, words, and behavior. This person is capable of manipulating people around them, especially those close to them to serve their selfish and self-fulfilling needs. They realize the fact that they can easily influence their partner and utilize this to the fullest by wielding control over their partner's actions.

In an addict-codependent relationship, the enabler is the passive codependent who willingly or unwillingly enables or fuels the manipulator's destructive behavior patterns. This is an attempt to comply with the manipulator to avoid what codependents view as displeasing or hurting them. The codependent will give up his/her values and identify to satiate the manipulator's needs. This can be a result of low self-esteem, insecurity, fear of being abandoned and several other factors. As a result of this, codependency creates a cycle of negative and destructive behavior patterns that are harmful to everyone involved, and can eventually destroy relationships.

Though not all codependent relationships involve addiction, addiction can worsen the codependency equation. Let us consider an example of a married couple where the wife is a drug addict and the husband is a caretaker or enabler. Despite living together for several years, the husband hasn't tried to get help for this drug abuser wife. Rather, he may purchase drugs for her, helps fund her habit and operates with the justification that if he doesn't get her the drugs, she will get it anyway. The codependent partner may try to feed the other person's addictions in a bid to protect them from harm. However, they fail to realize that both actions can be equally harmful. Whether she drives herself to obtain drugs or he sources them for her, both are damaging and risky. The codependent partner is deeply invested in the relationship, and believes he is doing the best to ensure his partner's attention, safety, presence, and affection. Nothing can be further from the truth, but this is typically the viewpoint codependents operate with. In the above example, while the wife is dependent on her husband for enabling her drug addiction, the enabler husband depends on the wife for obtaining his sense of self-worth, being needed and gaining her affection/attention.

This unfortunate cycle of codependency continues until something drastic halts it, usually hospitalization, grave illness or death. If you indentify with the patterns mentioned above, it may be time to seek professional intervention before the issue spirals out of control.

How are enabling and codependency linked? Enabling can be viewed as a behavior set, while codependency is the prime motive driving these behavior patterns. Codependency is a condition or mindset that feeds the tendency to indulge in engaging behavior. For example, engaging behavior is a codependent marriage may involve a spouse completely taking over the responsibilities and duties of the addict instead of attempting to rectify their actions. They may also cover-up or offer excuses for their spouse instead of making him/her accountable for their addictive behavior.

What are the typical signs of being in a codependent and enabling relationship with an addict? The biggest sign is the codependent partner or parent is giving up all other aspects of their life for the sole objective of attempting to protect the addict. The codependent partner or parent may lose sleep, stop eating and worry about their loved one in extreme ways. These are warning signs of codependency and enabling. In some cases, the codependent won't think twice before compromising their own values, ethics and moral code for protecting the addict. This violation of values constitutes enabling behavior to please the addict or go out of the way to protect them/cover up for them. Several codependents lie to protect an addicted spouse, parent or another family member.

If a person is constantly going against his or her own better counsel and values for accommodating the addict's behavior, it is most likely a sign of codependency. The most unfortunate part is the codependent knows that their behavior is wrong and often regrets it, but there's nothing they can do about it. They are almost addicted to covering up and protecting the addict from his/her own actions instead of helping him/her overcome the addiction. There is a deeply embedded subconscious belief that if the addict recovers from the addiction, he/she will no longer need the codependent. And not being needed is the worst nightmare of the codependent. Once their partner or parent breaks free from the addiction, the codependent believes he/she may not be needed, and hence their life will have no purpose. Thus, they unhealthily enable or fuel the addictive behavior to give a meaning or purpose to their life, which is caring for and being needed by the addict. They feed the addict's dependency on them in a bid to satisfy their own repressed and neglected emotions.

Codependency generally comprises dysfunctional actions that are similar to the addiction or abuse of the loved one, only the codependent partner is addicted to the addict. At times, partners, siblings, and parents may get so deeply involved with the addict that they tend to become dependent on the addict's need for them, and do not want to change the equation often at the cost of their partner's, sibling's or parent's sanity. Get the picture? Instead of setting boundaries and making the addict accountable for his/her actions, they give them a loose rope thinking the addict won't need them anymore, won't be able to functional normally or will be displeased if his/her addiction is stopped. Thus the enabling continues and assumes dangerous proportions in a relationship between two addictions, where one is addicted to a substance, alcohol and other similar elements while the other is addicted to a destructive relationship. This can be one of the most unfortunate codependent relationships ever.

Codependents mistakenly believe that they have to pick between putting up with their partner's (or parent's addiction) or watch them die. This makes them continue enabling behavior patterns when they know it is wrong or they may not wish to. All they want to do is help these addicts, and they see their enabling behavior as 'helping them' when it is the exact opposite. Even with the realization that their efforts are helping their partner, they compulsively go on with these enabling actions, eventually leading to highly damaging consequences for both. In such a scenario, the addict's guilt, powerlessness and hopelessness increase, and there is a serious loss of motivation when it comes to sobering up.

One way to tackle codependency and addiction is family therapy. It can help partners, siblings or parents identify the behavior patterns of their loved ones as well as their enabling behavior. In some complex cases, other conditions such as depression and emotional trauma can also cause addiction, which needs to be tackled through counseling and therapy. During therapy, you'll also learn of ways to recognize enabling behavior and different strategies to prevent it in the future.

There is hope and good news for codependents through intervention and treatment; however, it isn't until a crisis occurs that people opt for treatment. Codependency is also tricky to detect. You may not be aware of your codependency or may live in denial about a partner's addiction or abuse. Recovery and intervention are possible only when you acknowledge a problem exists by educating yourself and avoiding denial of the issue.

Begin by reading more about codependency, followed by opting for therapy, attending a multi-step program, counseling and other similar treatment plans. During the process of recovery, most therapists and counselors will attempt to shift the focus from your partner or parent to yourself. Much like codependency itself, its treatment also occurs in phases.

For instance, typically in the middle phase of codependency treatment, you will start building your identity, self-worth, self-confidence and the ability to assertively articulate your desires, emotions, and needs. You may learn to establish boundaries, express yourself freely and practice self-care.

Psychotherapy may involve tackling childhood trauma and/or healing PTSD. In the later stages of therapy and treatment, the codependent will focus on the idea that his/her happiness and sense of self-worth is not defined by other people or is independent of others. There is a greater sense of autonomy, independence, and self-reliance. This can help boost your intimate bonds, and help you enjoy more rewarding, fulfilling and gratifying relationships. You feel more powerful, in control and self-loved. There is a greater feeling of expansiveness, creativity, and productivity.

Thus if you are codependent and stuck in a relationship with an addict (or even a part of unhealthy codependent relationships), it may be time to seek professional intervention, counseling, and therapy to help you lead a normal, productive and rewarding life, while enjoying meaningful relationships.

Stages of codependency

Codependency isn't an ill that takes over your persona overnight. It is a slow, steady killer that is a result of reinforced behavior, your emotional situation, and coping skills. Codependency is often known as relationship addiction because a codependent is addicted to other people "wanting" or "needing" them. This, in essence, defines their purpose of existence or validates them. The focus is on alleviating your pain and hurt by concentrating on others. Codependents believe they derive their sense of well-being or happiness by caring about other people. However, ignoring ourselves only increases the inner pain and emptiness.

The underlying emotions that stay neglected make things worse over a period of time. These negative feelings grow to have even more harmful and damaging ramifications in the long run. The habit turns into a circular, addictive and self-perpetuating mechanism that assumes devastating effects. Despite being aware of the adverse consequences, the codependents' behavior becomes obsessive and compulsive.

This can take on several forms such as calling an ex partner we know we shouldn't be contacting or putting all our values and finances at stake to accommodate a partner's needs or stalking/snooping on a partner out of insecurity/jealousy. These are all extreme forms of codependent behavior where the codependent needs help. This is why it is referred to a disorder or addiction.

Here are the typical stages of codependency to help you indentify how it grows gradually yet insidiously, and takes over until you feel totally helpless and overpowered by it.

Codependency is a chronic condition with progressive and enduring symptoms, which means they worsen over a period of time if not subjected to proper treatment and intervention. Though its deeds are sown during one's formative childhood or adolescent years, it doesn't manifest until adulthood when a person becomes involved in close relationships. There are three clearly identifiable stages culminating into a growing dependence on an individual or relationship, and a parallel loss of focus and care of oneself.

The first stage – This stage looks like any other saccharine sweet romance with excessive attention, focus and dependency on the partner. There is an increased desire to please him/her. What makes it difficult to diagnose codependency at this stage is that almost every new relationship involves placing the other person on a higher pedestal and trying to please him/her all the time often at the cost of your own needs and desires. This may make it tough for you to view the condition as codependency upfront and objectively. However, in the case of codependents, there is a greater obsession with the individual. There is also a tendency to rationalize negative behavior (sometimes denying its existence), doubt one's own perceptions, failure to create or maintain boundaries and giving up your own individual life, activities or friends for pleasing or accommodating your partner. These are all symptoms of the early stage of codependency.

Middle stage – Slowly the codependent person increases their effort to minimize troublesome characteristics of the relationship, rather than acknowledge it. Thus, at this stage, self blame, regret, anxiety, frustration, and guilt begin to set. Over a period of time, your self-esteem and sense of self-worth take a backseat as you keep compromising yourself to accommodate the other person's needs and preserve the relationship. This leads to greater anger, resentment, guilt, and disappointment.

This is the stage during which codependents may withdraw from their friend circle and family. They take to hiding their problems, and not talking about their emotional grievances. There may be physical abuse, violence, conflict, verbal abuse, emotional withdrawal, and other issues. The codependent may use addictive mechanisms such as binge eating, shopping, substance or alcohol abuse and other similar destructive behavior patterns, habits or addictions.

Late stage – This is when the condition begins to take a toll on the codependent's emotional and behavioral well-being. It starts affecting their physical and mental health, often making them victims of stress induced disorders such as headaches, depression, anxiety, digestive problems, muscle pain, allergies, heart diseases and much more. The obsessive-compulsive behavior and other addictive behavior patterns increase over a period of time, thus leading to reduced self-care, self-confidence and self-esteem. There are growing feelings of frustration, despair, depression, anger, helplessness, and despair.

Codependency and dysfunctional families

A majority of dysfunctional families look perfectly healthy and normal from the outside, which makes it tough spot the negative elements. However, there can be plenty of internal relationship dynamics related to a family member's abuse, sickness, addiction, trauma and other similar reasons that can change the equation. Families can be dysfunctional owing to rigid or excessive control, emotional disconnection or absence of empathy. At times, there may be a lack of acceptance that can trigger codependency in children. The single largest cause for codependency, however, remains exposure to a codependent parent.

Codependency generally begins manifesting itself when a person experiences emotional or psychological abandonment. In response to lack of acceptance or abandonment by family members, he/she begins to repress their real emotions, needs, desires, and thoughts. There is an attempt to numb the pain and hurt, mistrust family members and become more self-reliant. In order to cope or get accepted, codependents conceal themselves behind a mask or false persona of strength. This leads to compulsive behavior that helps them cope with their repressed emotions for a while.

One of the biggest signs of a dysfunctional family is that it is often closed to different degrees. It doesn't exchange the creation of new ideas, free expression of thought or a healthy discussion among family members or outsiders. There is an unhealthy sense of rigidity, which children have a tough time breaking free from. For instance, some families may be terribly autocratic, dictatorial and intolerant, and not entertain friendships with people belonging to a certain religion or race. Other families may be totally disconnected from the community at large. Still, other families may be respected within the community but have plenty of hidden secrets that no one except family members know about. Such homes breed or create codependents. There is an underlying pattern of fear, shame, guilt and regret lurking around, which makes young children living in such households lose their confidence, repress their emotions, and look to shift away from focus from themselves to others in order to feel good about themselves.

Another symptom of a dysfunctional family is that family problems, issues and crises are never openly and freely spoken about. Parents often believe that the best way to deal with family issues is to stay normal and pretend the issue doesn't exist. The operating belief is that if you pretend something doesn't exist instead of taking it head on, it'll disappear of its own. Parents think living in denial about an issue will not expose their children to it, which means they (the children) won't notice or be impacted by it. However, pretending something doesn't exist makes things even worse for the children. Children often sense and notice that there is an issue, and the household authority's refusal to acknowledge it brings about an unhealthy inconsistency in their perceptions and denial or lack of acknowledgment of these perceptions by authoritative figures. This breeds lack of trust in parents and caregivers. At a young age, children may end up mistrusting their parents, and their own perceptions/feelings. They learn not to question people. This behavior continues when even as adults they doubt their own perceptions and avoid questioning people.

Denial of issues within the household implies to the children that it isn't healthy or good to talk about it, that frightening and painful issues are best neglected if you want to get over it. Codependency breeds when there is an issue which the family refuses to acknowledge. Parents or care-givers may pretend that a painful or hurtful truth doesn't exist within the household/family. They may attempt to act normally during a crisis. The issue never gets spoken about or addressed in a healthy manner, which leaves it unresolved. This sows seeds of doubt within children about their own perceptions, and they learn early on that they cannot talk about their fears, insecurities, and apprehensions, even within themselves. Denial of emotions and issues leads to repressed emotions, which often assumes the form of codependency when as adults the same children seek comfort from the pain of their own repressed emotions by caring for others.

Denial creates secrets. Some families end up hiding a potentially shameful and hurtful truth for several generations without acknowledging or talking about it even among family members. This secret can be related to violence, crime, sexual issues, addiction, and mental ailments. The guilt, shame, and regret are felt by children, however since no one talks about it, the children grow up confused and uncertain of their perceptions.

Even if they know the truth, they can't speak about it or raise questions about it, which ends up damaging their personality in the long run. This is precisely what makes codependency so challenging to overcome. The issues are often so deep seated and repressed that even the codependent isn't aware of it. Children in families that refuse to acknowledge their painful and shameful secrets often end up damaged, ashamed, unsure of their perceptions, low on confidence and anxious.

One of the biggest causes of codependency is learnt behavior. When we see an authoritative figure in the household reveal signs of codependency as children, we invariably internalize these destructive behavior patterns. This is why it is often stated that codependency is an 'inherited condition.'

Through observational learning, children learn to model their behavior on a codependent parent or caregiver. The basic premise is that children often learn behavior patterns by observing their role models than direct experience. A parent or caregiver's excessive helping behavior can gradually sow seeds of codependency in children that continue to impact their adult relationships. The parent's helping behavior influences the children's own excessive helping patterns, thus making them codependents in adult relationships. When we grow up observing caregivers and adults rescue, fix, enable and over care for another person, we end up identifying with these models or authoritative figures and following their destructive behavior patterns. This becomes even more impactful when we see others praising these family members, caregivers and authoritative figures for their ability to give so much of themselves to others. Later, these notions plant unhealthy ideas about giving in our formative minds, thus leading us to believe subconsciously that one is always responsible for looking after, rescuing, fixing and helping people often at the cost of our own happiness, sanity, and well-being.

What makes these learn behavior patterns so damaging is they are often internalized at a subconscious or unconscious level when we are too young to understand anything or have access to alternate ways of viewing the situation. We learn to accept this behavior and its consequences as the only truth while growing up. Thus, dysfunctional assistance becomes a familiar behavior pattern and the accepted routine. These ideas and notions stay unchallenged in our mind long enough to reveal themselves on our adult relationships.

We are subconscious driven to care for, rescue and fix things for others irrespective of the hazards associated with it. We simply learn that people we've grown up observing act like this in the given situation which must be the right way to act (in the absence of exposure to any alternative behavior patterns in a similar situation), and model our behavior on their codependent behavior. These patterns may continue for generations unchallenged until a person opts for family or counseling to break the pattern by identifying and acknowledging the issue of codependency.

Another typical trait of dysfunctional families is inconsistency, lack of uniformity and arbitrariness. Children don't know for sure when they'll be spared and when they will be punished. This makes rules confusing, senseless and unjust for them. It breeds cruelty, fear, uncertainty, insecurity, and apprehensions within them. There is a constant feeling of walking on thin eggshells, which makes these children grow into resentful, non-expressive and unpredictable adults. They end up believing that their identity, sense of self-worth and dignity gets violated. To restore their lost dignity, self-esteem, sense of self-worth and identity, they often take to caring excessively for or looking after other people.

Role confusion is another sign of a dysfunctional family. When a child is required to fill the role of a parent or assume parental responsibilities in the absence of a parent, the damaging seeds of codependency are sown. The child may become a caregiver/companion for their other parent or siblings, which makes them believe that they are always accountable and responsible for the family member's care, happiness, and well-being. This role is often fulfilled at the cost of their own needs, desires, and well-being. The scenario is common among divorced parents or where both parents lack emotional and/or physical intimacy. It ends up damaging the child's personality. The child is expected to act, feel and think like an adult according to the demands of the situation, which leads to the repression of their own feelings, needs, and emotions.

Unpredictability is another factor that can quickly unsettle children. If children know or can predict their parent's mood, it is easier for them to cope or adjust with the situation at home. However, unpredictability can make them forever anxious and fearful of how events will unfold next. Instead of becoming a safe and secure sanctuary, the home transforms into a battle zone that children seek to escape.

Inability to resolve problems and conflicts is another trait for a dysfunctional family. Resolving problems, challenges and conflicts are critical for the smooth functioning of a family. In dysfunctional families, though family members are constantly blamed and targeted for the same issues. There are either incessant arguments or silent resentment walls built over a period of time, both of which do little to tackle the issue from its roots. Things remain unresolved and end up impacting everyone including children.

Chapter Three: Why It Is Important to Place Yourself First

One of the most basic tips for being a part of healthy, positive, rewarding, meaningful and fulfilling relationships is putting yourself first. Now, this doesn't advocate selfishness, manipulation or showing scant regard for the other person's desires, needs, goals, preferences, and emotions. In a positive relationship, there is a healthy exchange of give and take. This means one isn't always playing the giver, while the other is perpetually the taker.

This isn't really about a "who cares for you?" stand in a relationship but more of "what do I want from the relationship?" A healthy relationship is about being as much assertive about your needs, desires, preferences, and goals as demonstrating concern for the other person's. In a codependent relationship, there is a tendency on part of the codependent partner to put their wants, emotions, and needs on the backburner to accommodate their partner's desires, needs, and emotions. Thus, there is a grossly unhealthy tilt of balance to favor one person.

Not being assertive when it comes to expressing your needs, desires, and preferences simply to avoid displeasing the other person or accommodating every their needs is not the sign of a healthy relationship. In a healthy relationship, you respect the other person's wishes, but equally demand that your wishes be respected too. Assertiveness is about arriving at a win-win situation, and not about placing one partner's needs above the other all the time.

Think of it like this, when there is a decision to be wielded from the mundane, daily stuff to the life transforming stuff, are you doing an internal check-in or simply going with whatever pleases your partner. An internal check-in can involve asking yourself if you are alright with the decision. So you have a say or opinion in the decision? Is it in the interest of both? Does it aligned to your value system or moral codes? Does it violate yours or your partner's needs, emotions, desires, and preferences? If you are simply focused on giving and more giving, you are burning yourself out. Respecting and valuing your needs and preferences don't necessarily imply discounting the other person's needs and preferences. Placing yourself first here implies respecting yourself enough to freely express your needs and desires, thus leading to a healthy assertion of your needs and values. You have to learn to respect, love and care for yourself before you learn to love, respect, and care for another person. A healthy self-esteem and sense of self-worth leads to more balanced and healthier relationships, where you aren't feeding the other person's harmful behavior to reinforce the purpose of your life or validate your presence in their life.

Some of the best relationship advice any relationship coach can offer you is placing yourself before the other person. Rather than terming this selfish and conceited behavior, understand its positive nuances. There is an underlying theme to most relationship suggestions dispensed in the present age, that you can't enjoy a fulfilling long-term relationship by becoming selfish. The notion is if one is selfless, one can't enjoy meaningful relationships. It sounds fantastically altruistic but doesn't work, especially when it comes to people who demonstrate codependent tendencies.

When you are healthy, happy, positive, productive and fulfilled, you contribute healthily, positively and productively to the relationship. If you are always playing second fiddle in the relationship, the frustration, misery, and displeasure build over a period of time before assuming damaging consequences. Without your own identity, opinions, preferences, sense of self-worth and independence, you will seldom be able to contribute positively to a relationship. Rather your actions, emotions, and behavior will be controlled by the other person. Having your own sense of identity, a healthy self-esteem and independent stand are integral to enjoying healthy, positive and fulfilling relationships.

People who put themselves first in the relationship and respect themselves enough to care about their needs, goals, desires, and preferences are happier and more fulfilled, which eventually helps them be a part of happier, positive and more fulfilling relationships. Repressing your feelings and emotions to accommodate the other person's needs is an unhealthy practice that can lead to negative consequences where the relationship is concerned, which is exactly what happens in a codependent relationship.

You keep repressing and underplaying your own wants, needs, and desires to avoid displeasing the other person or prevent them from abandoning you, thus leading to majorly unhealthy relationship practices that eventually spell doom for everyone involved.

Knowing, understanding, nurturing, loving and celebrating yourself is integral to the process of enjoying healthy and fulfilling relationships. You cannot be in a positive and healthy relationship if you don't feel good about yourself. In such cases, your sense of self-worth will be dictated by the other person. When you don't have an identity or a high self-esteem, you are making yourself vulnerable to be led where the other person wants to lead you, thus breeding codependency tendencies within you.

When you practice self-care, do the things you love doing and let go of a sense of obligation or compulsion that something must be done in order to feel loved, wanted and needed, you pave the way for more fulfilling and healthier relationships. Tune in to your inner voice to know what you want from the relationship and how to align your needs with the other person's. You will never need someone else to feed your sense of self-worth if you are confident with your own identity. Create an overflow of love, care, and joy so it can rub off on others associated with you.

When you start placing yourself first in the relationship in the relationship, you break away from the shackles of damaging habits almost instantly. What you do to yourself is what others will do to you – follow this rule and you'll seldom go wrong when it comes to enjoying positive and healthy relationships. Treat yourself the way you want others to treat you. If you want others to be more respectful towards you, start respecting yourself and your needs. The more you love yourself and discover your identity, the easier it will be for you to relate to others. The more you love yourself, the easier it will be for you give others love.

When you get better at looking after yourself or caring for yourself, you get better at looking after others. Avoid doing things out of a sense of obligation and compulsion. In healthy relationships, people don't do things for each other with an underlying sense of fear, insecurity or compulsion. They do things out of a sense of joy and fulfillment. Do things because you want to do it not because you'll something if you don't do it. In healthy relationships, people shower as much compassion on themselves as they do on the other person. Making yourself happy can start a positive and healthy self-reinforcement cycle. In a healthy relationship when one person is happy, the other person will invariably be happy too. Replace a sense of guilt and obligation with satisfaction, joy, and appreciation.

For instance, don't complete chores within the relationship out of a sense of obligation. This isn't the sign of a healthy relationship. Do it out of a sense of deriving satisfaction, joy, and appreciation from it. In unhealthy relationships, partners do things for each other out of a sense of fear, to prevent being abandoned by the other person.

Understand that every individual is a work in progress. You will never come with a 'completion date.' It is a continuous and ever-evolving process that involves knowing, understanding, loving, respecting and caring for yourself, which isn't the same as being selfish, manipulative and conceited in a relationship by always placing your needs and wants before the other person's.

Learn to be your own confidante, best friend, lover, and cheerleader before you can play the same role in someone else's life. Start by treating yourself the way you want to be treated by your partner. You don't have to necessarily be selfish, but become more mindful of staying aligned to your values, goals, feelings, preferences, and desires in a relationship.

In a healthy relationship, a person treats themselves with compassion, respect and care for others to take the clue and treat you in a similar manner. If you don't believe you are good enough, there's no way you are going to convince others to value you either.

Signs of a healthy relationship

I am often asked to elaborate on signs of a healthy relationship to help people determine if they are in one. If you are someone who is confused between signs of healthy and borderline unhealthy relationships, here are some indicators of a positive, healthy and fulfilling relationship.

Communication – communication is one of the most important factors of a healthy, meaningful and fulfilling relationship, especially in intimate relationships. In a healthy relationship, a person is freely able to express their wants, needs, desires, emotions, opinions, preferences, goals and dreams. There is no fear of displeasing or losing the other person by freely expressing yourself.

Communication is open, straightforward and healthy. One doesn't have to hesitate or think too much about what one says. Both partners feel comfortable opening up to each other with their innermost feelings and emotions. Good communication doesn't imply a lack of arguments. However, the couple is able to manage their differences more effectively. In a healthy relationship, there is nothing that can't be worked out through a healthy dialogue and exchange. Even if the partners disagree, they do so in a constructive manner.

In a healthy relationship, both partners feel safe communicating their needs, desires, and preferences. You are comfortable talking about potentially disturbing or sensitive issues with each other and set aside 'talk' time to address each other's communication needs. Listening is as important as speaking, which means giving the speaker complete and undivided attention is vital in a healthy relationship. In a healthy relationship, both partners can safely and comfortably express themselves without worrying about displeasing the other person or being abandoned by them for speaking out.

Accountability and responsibility – In healthy relationships, every person is responsible, answerable and accountable to their partner. This simply means accepting responsibility and accountability for their action and the effects instead of blaming someone or something else. It can mean owning their mistakes or admitting they screwed up. It doesn't imply that both have to constantly report to or check in on each other but admitting to and apologizing for your mistakes.

Boundaries – One of the biggest signs of an unhealthy relationship is lack of boundaries. A codependent relationship is often defined as one where a person fails to establish boundaries, owing to which their behavior is completely controlled by the other person. In order to please their partners, codependents fail to create and stick to boundaries, which lead to a serious breakdown in the relationship eventually. While it is important for the tow partners to spend time together, it is also vital for the relationship that they have independent lives.

Spending time apart, making new friends, pursuing new hobbies and taking up individual interests are vital for a healthy relationship. Be clear about what you will and will not do. In a healthy relationship, both partners are aware of each other's values and beliefs, and will not step on the other person's moral code to serve their selfish purposes. Both partners know what requests will be accommodated and what will be refused in a healthy relationship. There is no tendency to walk all over each other to fulfill serve manipulative and selfish needs.

Both partners in a healthy relationship have realistic expectations from each other and the relationship. Don't fantasize about unrealistic elements that can destroy the foundation of your relationship. A healthy relationship is not about fulfilling your fantasies but making the most of what you have. You are dealing with a real, complicated individual (much like yourself). This means there's already enough to work on without adding more unrealistic ideals to the equation.

Respect – Respect is one of the most important aspects in any healthy relationship. If you don't show respect for each other as partners and human beings, nothing else that's left in the relationship matters. Respect is integral to a healthy, positive and fulfilling relationship where both partners cherish, nurture and respect each other as individuals. In a healthy relationship, both respect each other's dignity, desires, preferences, and values.

In a healthy relationship, both partners are on the same plane where values and overall life goals are concerned. You both more or less want the same things from the relationship and life in general. There are common goals that you desire to accomplish together, and both are committed to accomplishing this goal collectively.

Support – A positive, healthy and nurturing relationship thrives on each other's support. You both should be there for each other during challenging times to encourage, inspire and boost each other's morale. Couples in a positive and healthy relationship often support and encourage each other when the waters run rough. A healthy relationship encourages both individuals to grow independently and together in the relationship.

Real love versus codependency

How do you know where real love ends and codependency begins? There can be a very thin line between the two as both are about fulfilling an inner need, being desired, caring for the other person and always being there to support a partner. However, while real love is positive, codependency is when this positive, genuine love assumes negative and dangerously obsessive forms.

The first major difference between real love and codependency is that the former isn't addictive. Of course, the first flush of romance can be highly irresistible but it doesn't take on unhealthy or damaging forms, unlike codependency where you are unhealthily consumed by the idea of caring for your partner's welling, playing rescuer, fixing things for them and basically disabling them from functioning without you. Real love isn't about being tied down to each other. Being tied down to each other originates from a feeling of fear, insecurity and low self-esteem. It is more codependency than real love.

While a surge of butterflies in the stomach and initial euphoria of true love or an intensely romantic relationship is healthy, it is replaced by completely focusing on the other person's needs in a codependent relationship. There is a loss of the sense of self, and the other person becomes the center of your universe in an unhealthy way.

While there is a healthy sense of self-worth, self-esteem, and self-confidence in real love, which allows a person to love other people as much as they love themselves, in codependent relationships, the love often stems from feelings of uncertainly, fear, insecurity, and anxiety. While real love is as much about caring for your needs and wants as the other person's, codependency is an unhealthy addiction about being needed all the time to fuel your own sense of self-worth.

At times people do not even realize that they are in a codependent relationship. They end up believing that their actions are driven by true love. They think it is a norm to love a person so much that you can't imagine how you ever existed without them. At the heart of it, real love makes you a better person. It increases your sense of self-worth and self-confidence by making you feel wanted and cherished. If your sense of self-esteem and self-worth is solely derived from the fact that a person needs you or clings to you all the time, it may be time to re-evaluate the dynamics of the relationship.

Avoid falling into the trap of confusing your relationship addiction for love. This is a complex process since the neuro-chemical responses for both are almost similar. Studies have revealed that exposure to visuals of our partner trigger the same reactions in the brain as those felt by cocaine addicts when they seek their fix to satisfy the craving.

Other than excitement and intense passion that marks both real love and codependency or addiction, real love is based on mutual trust, mutual respect, commitment, loyalty, compassion, and affection. Passion, excitement, and intensity alone do not define true love, though they are conspicuous in a codependent relationship.

Codependent relationships are underlined by inconsistency in affection, lack of emotional connection, unpredictable and erratic behavior by one partner just to keep the other partner on their feet. This just doesn't align with the notions of a healthy, positive or productive relationship.

Chapter Four: Recovery

When you know the typical characteristics of a codependent, unhealthy and destructive relationship, it is easy to identify one and take corrective measures in the right direction. Once you recognize and acknowledge that you are in a codependent relationship, it will be easier to tackle the condition. What are the typical signs of a codependent relationship? What are the general behavior patterns observed within a codependent relationship? The first step is accepting or acknowledging that you are in a codependent relationship. Recovery is possible only once you admit there is a problem. When you refuse to acknowledge the problem, there can be no remedial measures. If you are stuck in a codependent relationship, there are plenty of things you can do about it. However, most involve a huge shift in the way your mindset or the way you perceive yourself and tackling your emotions at a subconscious level.

Romantic codependent associations are generally characterized by a whirlwind, rapturous beginning. The two partners feel an intense attraction and passion, which is followed by enviable romance. The two people feel compulsively and hopelessly drawn to each other almost like there's no control. Most codependents believe that they've found their soul mate or that a higher force has brought them together. However, this feeling of euphoria is often short lived. As the relationship dynamics unravel, both partners may start developing a destructive attachment and dependence on others for defining their sense of self-worth. The codependent's life is entirely focused on their partner, with the tendency to make extreme sacrifices for accommodating their partner's needs or avoiding displeasing them. Everything is done with the intention of pleasing the partner, which helps the codependent feel needed and good about themselves.

Breaking away from the codependency cycle

Obviously, being in a codependent relationship isn't a very situation. It gradually yet steadily destroys your sense of self-worth and identity. The good news, however, is that codependency is a condition that can be overcome with persistence, determination and a strong will. Here are some practical, proven and actionable strategies for breaking free from the damaging cycle of codependency.

1. Avoid living in denial mode – One of the biggest obstacles for someone looking to free themselves from codependency is the inability to acknowledge that there is an issue in the relationship. At times, people spend their entire life in a codependent relationship without even realizing it. Other time, a codependent may mistakenly believe that they are in an interdependent relationship.

The first step towards taking remedial action against codependency in a relationship is to identify and acknowledge the issue. Denial encourages addiction. Irrespective of whether it is love, alcohol or cocaine, inability to indentify the issue is a sure fire route to increasing or feeding the addiction.

Codependents almost always exist in denial of their real issues. They refuse to recognize that there is an issue within the relationship that ought to be addressed and fixed. Codependents learn to repress their emotions, needs, and preferences to avoid rejection, abandonment, and criticism.

Watch out for the signs and symptoms of codependency described in the earlier chapters of this book. Do you indentify with a majority of these signs in your relationship? Do you feel like you are being controlled by your partner? Do you operate with a deep sense of insecurity, jealousy, unworthiness, inadequacy, low morale and a reduced sense of self-worth? Is your sense of self-esteem and self-worth fueled by being needed or wanted by others? Are you afraid of rejection and abandonment in a relationship and often go to any extent to avoid it? If you've answered yes to a majority of these questions, you may be in a codependent relationship, which means it is time to act immediately to identify and eliminate the condition.

2. Establish boundaries. One of the most common struggles of people in a codependent relationship is establishing precise and clear boundaries. If you are a people, struggling to be accepted and validated by others, it is going to be tough to say no to people. However, stop these attempts to please people, and establish clear personal boundaries in relationships.

There are certain things you will and won't do. Recognize where to draw a line, and ensure people respect it. People may attempt to manipulate you into doing precisely what they want by engaging in harsh words and actions. However, stick to your ground, and politely yet firmly state your response. Once you've made up your mind, do not change your stand. This will only encourage the manipulator to manipulate your behavior to suit their needs. Develop greater assertiveness to say no when you mean no. If it displeases people when you take the right stand, so be it. Understand that these people are merely preying on your feelings of inadequacy and insufficiency. Enforce limits in all relationships, especially in intimate relationships when you realize that you are in a codependent relationship. It will enable you to enjoy more positive, healthier and rewarding relationships in the future.

You need to bring about a change within the mindset to help you cut some slack on the people pleasing. Understand that you can please some people sometimes but not everyone, all the time. Given the fact that you cannot please everyone all the time, you will have to deal with the prospect of disappointing a few people. It is inevitable. Even if you do everything within your capacity to please someone, at some point you are going to disappoint them. Therefore, accept the fact that your actions are going to disappoint some people, and start looking out for your interests.

Again, understand that someone who is happy or pleased with you at some point may be disappointed with you at another point in time. Another person's validation of approval cannot be constant, and should not be used to boost your self-esteem or self-worth. Based on their interests and selfish objectives, other people's interests can be highly fickle and temporary. Don't let it drive your actions. It isn't a reliable spot to place your sense of self-worth or identity. If you base your sense of self or identity pleasing other people, it will keep changing according to the other person's whims and fancies.

Even if a person or people are pleased with you owing to the present pleasing behavior or actions, it doesn't imply that what you are doing is best for you. At times, something that feels wonderful in the short-term may not always be good for your long-term interests. Learn to gauge if what you are currently doing is beneficial for you in the short and long term. Self-direction requires time. If you invest efforts trying to win people over and keep their love, you are not spending enough time developing yourself or growing. Focus inwards rather than outwards. Work on sharpening your skills, progressing and improving your decision making abilities rather than spending time and effort trying to please others.

In codependent relationships, people get so absorbed and engrossed in the pursuit of caring for others that they begin neglecting or overlooking their own needs, desires, goals, and preferences. Once you realize that you are in a codependent relationship, you may want to quit the relationship. This decision may seem painful and unimaginable in the short-term but can have positive effects on your personality and emotional well-being in the long-run. Be firm in your resolve to walk out of the relationship. Before engaging in any discussion, stay firm that this is your decision, and it is exactly what you need. Prepare yourself for the fact that there is no room for negotiation and discussion. There is no scope for giving the relationship another shot.

There are high chances you've given the person or manipulator more chances than they deserve, without a change in their behavior. Though it may be relatively easier to break free from intimate or romantic relationships, you may not be able to break free from a sibling or parent. In such cases, the only option is to establish and enforce clear boundaries. When your behavior is consistent with the boundaries you've enforced, the person will realize over a period of time that you cannot be manipulated or controlled. Being firm in your resolve is the key. Once you decide to walk out of a codependent relationship or enforce boundaries, your decision should be non-negotiable.

Some codependent relationships may involve completely walking away from it, while other relationships may require you to step back and evaluate your needs, self-care, and development. At times, you may feel guilty about stepping down from your responsibilities, especially with regard to codependent relationships within the family. You may feel responsible for other people's actions or the need to go over your responsibilities. Setting limits about what you are willing and not willing to do becomes important in such a scenario. For instance, if your sister is hungover and wants you to call her workplace to offer some excuse on her behalf, be clear that this isn't something you will do for them. You can say something such as, "It wasn't my decision to get drunk last night. It is a result of your decision and action, and it is your responsibility to deal with the consequences of your actions." Assertive statements like these are important when it comes to establishing boundaries.

Let us take another example to understand this better. If you are engaged with an important assignment, and a friend calls up with his/her problems, what do you do if you have a codependent personality? On an instinctual level, you'll want to play savior to the friend and fix things for them. However, since you are involved in an important assignment, your time is crucial. Resist the urge to give in to lend them a sympathetic ear, and say something like, "I do care about your well-being and wish to offer support. However, it is also important for me to work on my assignment that is due tomorrow. Let us talk about this tomorrow.

If you want to establish clear boundaries, tell this to the other person. Say something like, "We may need to work out some issues but I am not willing to meet you in person. I want to limit our interactions only to text communication or conversations."

Detaching and detangling yourself from the relationship is critical to breaking free. It doesn't happen overnight. Gradually start disconnecting and distancing from things that cause you trouble. Avoid being preoccupied or over-involved with trying to fix, rescue, transform and control other people. Step back from the tendency to please people. One of the best ways to resist the urge to play savior all the time is to take a deep breath and let go things instead of trying to fix them. Acknowledge the fact that you cannot be around to fix every problem that occurs with the person. It isn't yours for fixing. Learn to differentiate between reasonable help and excessive dependence.

You don't have to feel responsible for others personally all the time. Understand that it is in the loved one's own interest that you do not accept responsibility for their comfort, safety, and well-being each time. By constantly trying to fix things for each, you snatch the opportunity to give them control of their own well-being and happiness. For your own selfish needs of being needed and wanted, you make them dependent on you, which is wrong at several levels. On the surface of it, it may feel like you are doing good for them by protecting them and looking after their well-being. However, in the long run, you are only reinforcing their dependence on others, thus disabling their power to take control of their life.

Indirectly, you end up sending the message that the person is totally helpless and powerless without you, and they aren't capable of looking after themselves. Eventually, the person starts believing this. The workaround for you this is to step back and help them take control of their life by focusing on your own life. Shift focus from their needs to yours.

Codependents often thrive on offering unsolicited advice and counsel to other people. Resist the temptation to offer unwanted advice however noble your intentions may be. You don't have to play agony aunt/uncle or counselor all the time. People, who feel the need to advice, guide and counsel others are deeply insecure, needy and lack self-esteem. Advising and guiding other people makes these people feel in control and boosts their own sense of self-worth. If you are excessively involved in the other person's life, actions and decision making, there is a chance you are treading on their personal boundary. Respect and honor healthy boundaries that help the person and relationship grow.

Learn to speak the truth instead of forever being a "yes" person. One of the biggest challenges codependents struggle with is the inability to say no to their partner (or parent, friend, sibling etc.) for fear of displeasing them. Displeasing or hurting people is the last thing they'll do because they fear the displeased person will abandon them.

Consciously start developing the habit of saying no when you actually mean no. Don't say yes when you mean no. Also, learn to be frank and express your true feelings instead of trying to please people by saying yes all the time. Don't smile and pretend nothing happened when you are actually upset with the person. Admit they caused you pain/hurt, and confront them about it. Start acknowledging and expressing your true feelings by talking about things as they are! This is a good starting practice for liberating yourself from the vicious cycle of codependency. Don't hold back your emotions because you think it will cause problems. Understand that you are working towards resolving a long-term problem. Be gracious, polite and open-minded while expressing your feelings. Find healthier and more positive ways to discuss potentially sensitive issues.

One thing that I'd like to reiterate here is, when you identify that you are in a codependent or manipulative relationship where you've been taken advantage of, do not criticize, blame, humiliate or insult your partner. Labeling and name calling makes it worse. Calling out someone for being mean, inconsiderate and selfish for not spending enough time with the family doesn't solve the purpose. Instead, you can say something like, "when you don't spend time with is, we feel neglected."

3. Work to realign your views about abandonment. One of the biggest reasons codependents assume the role of a helper or caretaker is because they believe having someone dependent on them or increasing someone's dependence on them will prevent that person from abandoning them. This feeling of being abandoned may be closely connected to a traumatic childhood incident or being abandoned by caregivers during your formative years.

If you operate with the fear and insecurity of people leaving you, you may consider professional intervention or counseling. A therapist can help bring about a change in your perception about yourself and work on eliminating your underlying fears to help you perceive other people and relationships in a different light. Explore different ways to practice self-care and trust other people. If you want to free yourself from codependency tendencies, in the long run, you may want to actively work on the fear of being of being abandoned. These fears, apprehensions, anxieties, and insecurities are so deeply entrenched with our subconscious that it becomes near impossible to identify and challenge them without professional intervention. When you have a deep seated fear but don't know its origins or are unable to cope with it despite knowing its origins, you may need to opt for therapy.

Seeking validation for your sense of self-worth or self-esteem from others needs to be stopped immediately when you identify you are in a codependent relationship and want to break free from it. No one has to tell you that you are important to them. That sense of validation and self-worth should originate from within you and not externally. You don't need others to increase your sense of importance. You can be your own cheerleader in a positive and healthy way.

As you are contemplating ending the relationship, introspect about where your sense of self-esteem and self-worth come from. How do you see yourself? How would you describe yourself? What are your views, thoughts, and perceptions about yourself? What are your perceptions and ideas about everything you deserve and don't deserve? You may want to reevaluate or rework on your perceptions about yourself because, in a majority of codependent relationships, the underlying issue is a faulty or negative self-perception.

As a codependent, you may be focused on other people's needs and overlook your own needs, desires, goals, and preferences. Codependents often dedicate a huge chunk of their time to caring for the other person often at the cost of self-care. Your entire identity may be based on caring for another person. There may be absolutely no identity beyond caring for the other person. Start taking stock of your needs. For example, do you need time for rejuvenating and recharging following a stressful day? How do you cope with or manage stress? In your bid to care for the other person, have you ignored your own nutritional needs, physical activities and sleep? Begin to regain a sense of your needs by building a self-care schedule.

One characteristic of codependents is that they tend to repress or hide their emotions. Don't pretend everything is alright when it isn't. If there are issues related to a painful childhood, unexpressed emotions and fear of abandonment, acknowledge them. Be more mindful and conscious of your feelings. Reflect upon the relationship and the sense of self-worth and identity you derive from it. How do you feel about and in the relationship?

Avoid ignoring or overlooking your emotions because you don't want to be honest with yourself or are living in denial. One of the things that work wonderfully well when it comes to freely expressing your emotions is writing a journal in the flow of consciousness.

Simply pour your feelings on paper in an unrestrained manner. Through the process of penning down your true emotions, you may end up accessing your deepest, innermost feelings that you didn't even know existed. You may want to write about your sense of identity, childhood experiences and emotions attached to the current relationship.

Freely express yourself and tap into your emotions, which will help you identify emotions and experiences that are holding you behind in codependent relationships. You may also want to maintain a dream journal to observe a pattern of feelings, emotions, and ideas held in the subconscious mind. It may reveal your deepest fears, insecurities and other emotions. Simply keep a dream journal beside your bed, and note each dream in as much detail as you can immediately upon awaking.

At times, we aren't of the destructive or self-limiting emotions and experiences that are holding us behind. Identifying a pattern can help us break free from this negative cycle. You can also open up about bottled or repressed emotions to a trusted friend or therapist. Acknowledging these feelings is critical to the process of recovering from codependency. Regain a sense of your own needs, desires, priorities, interests, preferences, and goals.

The first and most important step for breaking free from the cycle of codependency involves taking an objective look at the past to identify, understand and reveals emotions and experiences that may have led to the codependency. What is your family background and history? Why type of a home and family did you grow up in? Was there emotional neglect or physical, emotional and/or verbal abuse? Were there specific events or circumstances that drove you to disconnect yourself from your real feelings and emotions, while overlooking your own needs and priorities?

This is one of the toughest processes when it comes to overcoming codependency. Reliving a painful childhood can be tough. You may find yourself going over painful emotions such as anger, frustration, guilt, regret, and sorrow. However, this is integral to the process of recovery. Think of it as a thorn that's stuck in your skin. It will keep hurting you until you show demonstrate courage once and for all to remove the thorn and experience intense pain for a short time in exchange for a lifetime of freedom from it.

However painful acknowledging these feelings and emotions may seem on the surface of it, it is vital to the process of coming out of these self-limiting emotions and realigning your perception about yourself. Self-exploration can be stressful, painful and emotional but it's the first step towards taking control of your life and relationships by moving out of codependent relationships.

Identify denial. Once you recognize painful emotions and childhood experiences that led to the codependency, be frank when it comes to accepting or talking about your initial denial. You may have pretended there is no problem in the relationship. In some instances, even gone ahead and justified or rationalized the codependency over a period of time. Admit that you've been a part of a codependent relationship and denied it for long. View the relationship for what it is – dysfunctional. Being honest with yourself is the key to enjoying positive, healthy and fulfilling relationships in the future.

4. Practice self-care – Give up the idea of trying to please everyone and start focusing on self-care and self-development. The right people will be naturally drawn to you if you show yourself the same care, respect, and affection that you give others. Healing from codependent relationship/relationships can be a long and challenging process. Start with small self-care measures that allow you to focus on yourself over others.

Begin by becoming more aware of your feelings, emotions, thoughts, priorities, and needs. Take care of your own needs. Self-care involves looking after yourself physically, emotionally and spiritually. Eat healthy meals, get restful sleep, stick to an exercise or physical activity routine, take any prescribed medication of time and visit a doctor if required. These are needs that are often overlooked by codependents while caring for the other person.

Look after your mental and emotional well-being. Make new friends and social connections, join hobby clubs and connect with people who have similar interests as you. Explore positive activities that give you happiness and some much needed emotional downtime. You may want to spend time meditating to get in touch with or evaluate your thoughts, emotions, beliefs, values, opinions, needs and desires.

Be more compassionate towards yourself. Treat yourself with the same kindness, care, and love that you extend to others. Here is a little practical exercise for codependents to practice self-compassion.

Start by sitting in a relaxed position in a comfortable, positive and disturbance free setting. Close your eyes. Visualize you're a friend you care deeply about. Imagine that this friend is really devastated, and reaching out to you. They may be hurting because of a relationship gone wrong or losing their job or failing at something. The equation of their life seems totally altered. What would you tell them at such a time? "This isn't really your fault because you had nothing to do with this" or "You did your best but these things are not in our control and we must deal with it." Would you say something like, "Of course it's your fault, you should have done this instead of that" or "You really didn't try harder" or "This happened because you were not talented, good-looking and smart." No right? If you wouldn't say it to a friend you deeply care about, why you would say it to yourself?

The most likely approach when a friend comes to you with a problem will be hugging them and consoling them by saying it isn't their fault and things will get better. "I am really sorry you have to face this, what can I do to make things better for you?" You should demonstrate the same kindness, affection, and compassion for yourself. Start by saying things to yourself that you would say to a close friend. Avoid saying anything that you wouldn't ever say to a loved one. Treat yourself with the same compassion that you would extend to a friend in trouble. Challenge any negative thoughts, self-criticism and negative notions about yourself that have defined your sense of self-worth for long. Alter your perception, and learn to value yourself.

When you spend more than a healthy share of time and efforts trying to please or win other people's approval, you may not be spending sufficient time working on yourself. Tap into your inner feelings, emotions, and intuitions to work on your ability to control your actions and take independent decisions.

5. Heal with mindfulness and meditation – Mindfulness and meditation is a wonderful way to tackle the monster of codependency head on. Healing from codependency starts when we look after and care about for ourselves, and what better way to show your body, mind, and spirit some care than meditation. Start by identifying and acknowledging your situation. When you tell yourself there is a problem that needs to be resolved, you start working on a solution actively.

Show yourself some much needed compassion and love with meditation. Establish an intention to act, think and feel differently. Meditation and mindfulness are power-packed healing tools. They help in decreasing stress, anxiety and frustration. These disciplines also help us become less reactive, and more in control of our thoughts, feelings, and emotions. Meditation and mindfulness offer hope and allows us to focus on what matters rather than being distracted by the negative situation around us. A daily, consistent and committed practice of meditation will help you understand, acknowledge and identify your needs. Among other things, you will learn detachment, relaxation, self-compassion, joy, and self-care.

Mindfulness helps us gather control of our thoughts, feelings, emotions, and mindset, which can help in reprogramming our innermost emotions and thoughts. To break free from the negative cycle of codependency, a person needs to bring about a shift in the perception of the self. You need to realign or reprogram your thoughts from negative to positive. Mental chatter and internal self-talk have to transform from critical to more hopeful, balanced and encouraging.

Meditation and mindfulness help us gain greater control of our thoughts, feelings, ideas, and emotions. To practice mindfulness, it is important to observe, practice, participate and absorb the present moment in a non-judgmental and purposeful/intentional manner. Mindfulness helps us know and understand ourselves better. It also helps us monitor and control our reactions in specific situations. Codependent individuals tend to exhibit compulsive behavior without much thought or awareness about the ramifications of their actions or surroundings. The emotions of the codependent are closely entwined with the other person that they fail to distinguish between where their feelings and emotions stop, and other's begins.

Find a serene, relaxed, comfortable and distraction free place. Relax your back, neck, limbs, and shoulders. You can either be seated in the floor or on a chair. Take a couple of deep breaths, and stay in the moment.

Start with awareness of the breath. Observe your breathing pattern by focusing all your attention on the breath until your mind is able to laser concentrate on a micro area by blanking out all other thoughts and distractions. This won't come immediately, especially if you aren't a habitual meditation practitioner. It will take some time, effort and discipline, but eventually, you'll learn to focus on the breath by eliminating all other distracting thoughts, ideas, and feelings.

The objective is to completely immerse yourself in the current moment by viewing it in a non-judgmental and intentional manner. There's no past or future, you only focus on the present moment and everything it brings. Slowly inhale and exhale. Take deep breaths, and focus only on the breath. Feel a surge of oxygen entering your mouth, throat, lungs, chest, and abdomen. Focus only on the process of breathing in and breathing out, while clearing the mind of all disturbing and distracting thoughts. When a thought occurs, briefly acknowledge it and let it pass.

Do not attempt to push the thought out of your consciousness. It will make the thought come back with greater force. Simply acknowledge it and allow it to live its time before fading away. The process should be natural, not forced.

Next, begin to observe and scan the entire body beginning from the head, going right down to the toe. What are the sensations experienced within each body part as you breathe? Each thought, feeling, and emotions that occupies our minds is accompanied by a matching physical sensation. The problem arises when we become so unhealthily imbalanced and disconnected with ourselves that we lose the ability to fully experience our emotions and accompanying physical sensations.

Equanimity is another important aspect of mindfulness. Through equanimity, you can evaluate your success. We have the tendency to escape from unpleasant or discomfort causing thoughts while chasing more pleasant and positive ones. When something good happens to us, there is a pattern of developing more desire, craving and clinging tendencies towards it. We seek even more of this pleasant thing.

The problem begins when we are unable to get enough of this pleasant thing we crave. This leads to frustration, misery and a feeling of hopelessness. Similarly, we desire to stay away from unpleasant things and situations. When these things occur, again our feelings of hopelessness, misery and frustration increase.

This habit pattern develops when we recognize our power as children, and start wielding control over our environment. Though we feel we are in control, our surroundings quickly take over and control us. Equanimity is an important skill and pattern that trains codependents to get back lost control, develop emotional and psychological contentment, and experience serenity.

Meditation helps restore your sense equanimity to help you develop greater awareness, psychological stability and increased composure that is unruffled by experience or exposure to unpleasant emotions, hurt, pain and other ills that can cause a personal to lose their mental balance. You develop greater control of emotions, and mental calmness even in the face of unpleasant emotions, thoughts, and circumstances.

6. Practice visualization – Another wonderful way to reprogram your subconscious mind is visualization. Codependency often involves holding

negative emotions, self-limiting beliefs and traumatic experiences in the mind (some of which you may not even be aware of). To beat the monster of codependency, you have to bring about a shift in your innermost feelings, beliefs, ideas and thoughts about yourself, and the type of relationship you really want. The best way to reprogram your subconscious mind from negative to positive is to feed it with greater positivity using your imagined ideal.

Once you acknowledge that there is an issue, you will realize that the relationship isn't exactly what you wanted or things haven't gone as you had imagined. There are issues and emotions you'd been neglecting over a period of time. Now, shift the focus away from what you don't want and instead focus on what you want.

In explicit detail, complete with sensory experiences, visualize everything you seek in a relationship. Imagine your ideal partner – how does he/she look? What does he/she wear? What are the feelings and emotions he/she triggers in you? How do they contribute towards your progress and development? How do they make you feel about yourself? How they help in boosting your sense of self-esteem and self-confidence?

What makes visualization such a powerful exercise is that it realigns and brings about a shift in the thoughts, emotions, and feelings held within the subconscious mind. The reason most life coaches, self-help gurus, counselors, and therapists work with our subconscious and unconscious mind is that there is a little-known secret about it.

Our subconscious mind cannot distinguish between imagined reality and reality, which means it ends up accepting all the images and visuals you feed into it as real. When you imagine your ideal relationship and partner, it believes it to be your reality. Similarly, when you imagine being valued, respected and cared for by your partner, the subconscious mind picks up these powerful images as reality.

Thus over a period of time, these images are firmly embedded into your subconscious mind as your reality. When your mind believes these images to be your reality, it directs your actions in line with this reality. Your actions are more in alignment with discovering your ideal mate and enjoying a rewarding relationship.

Though visualization can be practiced anytime, the best time probably is just before you go to bed since our subconscious mind is most active when the conscious mind is resting. We "sleep over our problems" because our active subconscious mind allows us to experience ideas, thoughts, insights, and solutions that are beyond the realm of the conscious mind. Early mornings are also a good time to practice visualization exercises. Be seated in a comfortable, relaxed, positive and distraction free place, where you are not likely to be disturbed for the next 10-15 minutes. Close your eyes. Begin with mindful breathing or focusing on the breath before moving to imagining everything you want to become and seek from your ideal relationship. Even you will be blown away by what your mind is capable of imagining.

Back up your visualization exercises by setting goals about becoming your visualized, ideal self, and enjoying healthy, happy and positive relationships. Much like all other issues in life, there's no elevator on the way to recovery from codependency. You'll have to work your way through the stairs, gradually and steadily.

Visualization exercises for reprogramming the subconscious mind can also be complemented by the use of a vision board. A vision board is a regular board that has pictures of your dreams, goals, desires, and ideals stuck on it. Use images from the internet, magazines, brochures or just about anywhere to make your vision board as personal, meaningful and relevant as possible. It has to represent everything that you want in life. You may stick pictures of your ideal partner or a happy couple. You may stick images of a confident, self-assured and talented celebrity who you aspire to be like. How about pictures of a famous couple you admire or look up to as the ideal relationship?

Your vision board (also known as the dream board) represents everything you desire in yourself and the relationship. You can make it as attractive, relevant, meaningful and personal as possible by complementing the images with your favorite quotations, movie dialogues, motivational phrases and lines from your favorite book. Use stickers, sketches, sparkle and just about anything to make your vision board 'wow.' Place it in a prominent place where you can see it before going to bed and immediately after awaking so the images are firmly imprinted in your subconscious mind.

7. Get over the victim mindset – One of the first things you'll have to do to shake off the codependency mindset is to feel more in control rather than be controlled. This means getting out of the victim mindset and beginning to take control of your life and relationships.

There are several unconscious forces that come into play owing to the beliefs developed during our early childhood years. For instance, if we grow up with a shame or guilt based self-concept that we are failures or undeserving of happiness, our unconscious beliefs prevent us from accomplishing success irrespective of the efforts we put in.

These self-limiting beliefs are usually the result of growing up in dysfunctional families where abuse, excessive control, lack of communication, addiction and closed systems are a norm. Abusers often exercise control over their partner through manipulation tactics such as undermining them or inducing feelings of guilt. Control may also take serious form with direct threats or using children as a means for blackmailing one's spouse. All these negative experiences can lead to the codependent feeling like helpless victims.

To overcome codependency, you have to shed the victim notion and feel empowered. You have to take back the reigns of your life that were being controlled by other people until now. Learn everything you can about the situation you are in currently. Information gives you power. Next, you may want to seek an appointment with a therapist or opt for counseling to get out of the victim mindset. Observe other people's undesirable behavior and your reaction to it more objectively. Avoid the urge to react to everything even in the face of extreme provocation. Ask yourself if reacting to it makes you feel good or stops the undesirable behavior? Experiment with varied responses that evaluate the result.

Determine objectively if you are aligned with your values, dreams, and goals. What steps can you take to align with your dream life, ethics, values, and goals? Take measures to meet your unmet needs. Is there something you've wanted to do for long but couldn't because owing to the codependent relationship? What are the core beliefs that are holding you back from accomplishing your goals? These are questions you must answer and act upon to feel more empowered.

Accept responsibility and accountability for your actions, choices, and decisions. Being accountable for your actions is the first step towards free yourself from the victim mindset and accepting greater responsibility. Start saying, "I desire to" or "I wish to" instead of "I am compelled to" or "I must do this" or "I have to do this." This makes you feel more in control of your actions. It makes you feel like you choose to do something instead of being forced to do it.

Next, take action. Simply changing your mindset to one of greater empowerment doesn't serve your purpose unless it is backed by positive action. Gain the required skills and abilities to accomplish your goals. For instance, if you nag you're your partner to repair something and they keep refusing to do it, acquire the ability to do it for increasing your own sense of independence.

Learning to be on your own by developing the necessary skills is vital to the process of breaking free from codependency, and being more in control of your life. If lack of skills, education, vocational training etc. is preventing you from getting a job or building your own income, sign up for the required classes.

Learn to develop greater assertiveness. This will empower you to be more truthful, establish limits and build your sense of self-worth. Understand that no one but you are responsible for your happiness and unhappiness. The remote control for your feelings, emotions, thoughts, ideas, and beliefs is with you.

Do not start narrating incidents or accounts of your relationships in a manner that paints you as the victim. This will only end up reinforcing your ideas and beliefs of hopelessness, being controlled and helplessness. It further embeds the victim syndrome in your psyche, thus limiting your ability to break free from the cycle of codependency. Pay conscious attention to your thoughts, emotions, feelings, and words. What are your thought patterns? Are you unknowingly using words, phrases, and narratives that portray you as the victim? Be more proactive in your approach. Avoid playing the role of a reactive victim who is constantly subjected to situations that are beyond your control. Operate with the belief that you are the only force that can make things happen for you. The key to unlocking your happiness, well-being, success, and self-confidence is in your hands alone. Everything you seek and desire to accomplish is within you, and you don't need to seek external support for validating yourself.

Another way to break free from the unfortunate cycle of codependency is to enlist unconditional support from trusted friends and family members who accept you for exactly what you are. Do not be afraid to reach out to the right people for help, encouragement, and support when you feel stuck in a codependent relationship. These positive connections will make your process of transitioning from the role of a victim or constant rescuer to a normal, emotionally healthy individual much smoother.

8. Use affirmations – Affirmation are positive and powerful statements that are integral to your recovery process. These positive words when chanted or said in a loop imprint the right ideas to your subconscious mind, which then directs your actions in the right direction. The beliefs we hold in our own unconscious forces shape our perspective, which eventually determines the nature of our relationships.

To change or transform our relationships, we must first attempt to change our equation or relationship with ourselves. Bring about a change in your beliefs, attitudes, and mindset by using feeding your unconscious forces with positive affirmations. Affirmations should also be said in present tense, as if what you desire is already your reality. Also, avoid using negative words and phrases like "not", "do" or "do not.' Replace these negative terms with positive words and phrases to make your affirmations even more effective.

Without even realizing it, our mind is often filled with negative and self-limiting chatter. It happens so involuntarily that we fail to recognize it or put an end to it. This negative self-talk then grows into more damaging and harmful self-beliefs, which eventually leads us to codependent behavior. What makes the negative self-talk and criticism so powerful is that we often believe what we tell ourselves. By using positive affirmations, you can change the frequency of your thoughts from negative to positive. Repetition of these positive affirmations helps you reprogram your inner beliefs and ideas to alter the way you perceive a situation. Thus you can recondition your mind to accept more positive and empowering ideas. Positive affirmations help you focus on the positives rather than negatives in any situation.

Here are some affirmations that can facilitate the recovery process for codependents.

I am a wonderful and magnificent being who is filled with love, positive energy, and light.

The light and fire inside me are capable of creating plenty of miracles in my life.

I am in a natural state of abundance. I open embrace and welcome it in my life.

I hold the power to transform all my experiences and circumstances into opportunities for greater clarity, focus, and power.

I deserve to be loved, valued, cherished and celebrated in a relationship.

I deserve to be in a loving, caring, nurturing, healthy and positive relationship.

The universe loves, nurtures, desires and conspires to help me win all the time.

I am beautiful, radian, joyful, healthy and vibrant.

I deserve to be happy, in control, successful and productive

I make my own decisions, circumstances, and choices.

I have the freedom to choose how to live and I give priority to my desires, preferences, care, happiness, and well-being.

Irrespective of my circumstances and situations, I choose my well-being and happiness. My happiness and well-being are in my hands.

I am a confident, assertive, self-assured and productive individual who is able to live freely.

I am in a healthy, happy, fulfilling, nurturing, gratifying and productive relationship.

I deserve to be loved unconditionally.

9. Learn to embrace your imperfections – One of the major causes of codependency is our inability to come to terms with our imperfections, and the resulting feelings of being unworthy or undeserving. Understand that while chasing excellence may be a good thing, an obsession with perfection can have harmful consequences. It is an unrealistic, irrational and unrelenting expectation that you should be wonderful at everything to be loved and respected. You can't say or do the right thing all the time. Codependents are often unable to form a healthy idea about perfection.

It is more often than not used by them for feeling worthy, desired and in control. The issue arises when we have unrealistic expectations of ourselves as well as other people. There is bound to be disappointment, despair, and frustration.

We have to deal with plenty of unmet needs, unfulfilled expectations and a host of problems they bring along. It can assume several forms ranging from the mean inner critic raring his ugly head to being more rigid in our thought patterns to resorting to all or nothing catastrophic thinking to ruminating. Other extreme forms of struggling with perfectionism may result in anxiety, depression and other mental disorders.

Most people who are a part of codependent relationships have grown up in families that lacked safety, security, and predictability. As a result of this, they underplay their anxiety by trying to control everything around them. Being perfect becomes a way a life for codependents to prevent the other person's rejection, abandonment and criticism. There is a notion that being perfect will make us more worthy of being loved and respected, or in the least, we will not be hit, rejected or abused. To move out of the cycle of codependency, drop your desire to be perfect. Don't be obsessed with the need to be the perfectionist savior or rescuer all the time. Instead focus on being more mindful of meeting your needs, beliefs, desires, and values in a relationship.

Unhealthy emotions such as shame, guilt, and regret are often at the root of this quest for perfection. There is an operating belief in almost every codependent, that something is terribly wrong with them or that they aren't good enough. It is at the root of both – an obsession with perfection and codependency. Thus, codependents attempt to offset their so-called inferiority or unworthiness by trying to be perfect. However, this quest for perfection becomes a thorn in the feet of the codependent. The greater their obsession with perfection, the more unworthy and undeserving they end up feeling about themselves.

Understand that your mistakes, regrets, and problems aren't evidence of your unworthiness or inferiority. Everyone has their share of problems, blunders, guilt, shame, and regret, which doesn't make them unworthy. See your mistakes, problems, and challenges as normal to get away from the cycle of perfectionism and codependency. Learn to talk about your mistakes, regrets, and struggles with trusted friends in a healthy and positive manner than sweeping it under the carpet. This will allow you to confront your mistakes and see them for what they are rather than resorting to catastrophic thinking.

Understand the fact that perfectionism doesn't create a high self-esteem. As a perfectionist and codependent, you will only end up attempting to prove your point all the time just to feel wonderful about yourself. This doesn't tackle the issue from its roots. The notion helps by perfectionist codependents that perfection alone is the path to happiness and worthiness is false and should be challenged.

Avoid being too harsh on yourself and set realistic goals. By setting realistic goals, you will be able to accept and love yourself just the way you are. When you love and accept yourself unconditionally, it is difficult for others to follow suit. You don't have to go out of the way to do things for people just to earn their acceptance, love, and validation in return. When you accept yourself for what you are rather than being obsessed with perfection, you'll stop craving the need to be needed by others all the time, which will slowly but surely help you detach yourself from codependent relationships. You will stop doing things to please others or make you feel great about yourself because you already know what you are.

Do not be too hard on yourself. Forgive yourself for past mistakes and imperfections, while demonstrating greater compassion, self-love, and self-acceptance. Silence your inner critic, and replace it with more positive words and phrases that do not make you feel like an unworthy moron. Kindness and compassion is the key to freeing yourself from codependent relationships. It won't happen overnight. It's a gradual yet effective process that begins with accepting yourself as you are without wanting to change anything about yourself.

Stay more realistic when it comes to setting expectations from yourself and others. This will lead to fewer unmet needs and a greater sense of well-being. The road to contentment involves aligning our expectations with a healthy sense of reality.

Conclusion

Thank you once again for downloading this book. I hope the book gave you some invaluable insights and empowered you with the required information to help you feel more confident about overcoming codependency.

The next step is to implement the strategies given in this book. All the information you arm yourself will have little value if you don't put it to work. Everything works if you make it work. We hope you are able to enjoy more enriching and rewarding relationships in the future.

If you enjoyed reading this book, please take some time to share your amazing thoughts by posting a review on Amazon. We'd love to know your experience with the book and how it helped you. It'd be highly appreciated.

Made in the USA
San Bernardino, CA
08 November 2019